Creating a
Healing Society

For Robert —

It was a pleasure
to meet you in
santa Fe. I hope
you enjoy this
book.

Sincerely
Susan

For Sharon
With love, respect, and gratitude

Creating a
Healing Society

The Impact of Human Emotional Pain and Trauma
on Society and the World

Susan Lawrence, M.D.

www.CreatingAHealingSociety.org

Elite Books

Santa Rosa, CA 95403

www.EliteBooksOnline.com

Library of Congress Cataloging-in-Publication Data

Lawrence, Susan. (Susan E.)

Creating a healing society : the impact of human emotional pain and trauma on society and the world / by Susan Lawrence.

p. cm.

ISBN-13: 978-1-60070-021-7

ISBN-10: 1-60070-021-7

1. Psychic trauma. 2. Psychic trauma—Social aspects. I. Title.

BF175.5.P75L39 2006

155.9'3—dc22

2006028110

Copyright © 2006, Susan Lawrence

Cover design by Lightbourne

Typesetting by Karin Kinsey

Edited by Kenneth Hartman

Copyedited by Melissa Mower

Images used with the kind permission of emerson Matabele

Typeset in Hoefler Text

Printed in USA

First Edition

10 9 8 7 6 5 4 3 2 1

At first people refuse to believe that a strange new thing can be done, then they begin to hope it can be done, then they see it can be done—then it is done, and all the world wonders why it was not done centuries ago.

—Frances Hodgson Burnett

Acknowledgements

This book has been evolving within me for a very long time: longer, perhaps, than one might believe possible. If not for certain people in my life, I would not have been able to write it in its current form, much less let anyone else read it. I would like to honor these people here.

Sharon Tobin, my therapist, mentor, and friend: My deepest gratitude to you for walking with me on my journey of healing from trauma; for being present with me in times of great anguish and despair; and for helping me find clarity and peace.

In memory of Sonny Bartz, my beloved husband and friend: You gave me the precious gift of showing me how to live in the world, and changing my view of the world forever.

In memory of Frank Altadonna, my best friend and life partner: In my time of greatest need, you were there for me, even on the other side of death; I am in awe of your immense capacity to love.

Christian Bartz, my extraordinary grandson: I love and respect you so much, my wise and compassionate teacher.

Dave Mashore, my dear friend, colleague, and partner in creating a healing society: Thank you for your tireless efforts to bring healing to the world; for your wisdom and insight; and for the wonderfully descriptive phrase, "mushy middle."

Ken Hartman, my brilliant editor: I am so grateful for your presence in my life; if not for you, this book would never have been published.

Contents

Foreword

Where do we start in order to make a safer, more just and peaceful world? Do we wait until we reach stardom to offer up our "causes"? Do we take our concerns to our elected officials or to the United Nations? Do we manufacture bumper stickers to save the whales, curse the Republicans, dismiss the liberals, or promote religion? Do we descend into apathy because our arena is too small to make a difference in this chaotic and dangerous world of ours? Where do we start?

Many of us never start, as we are too busy just surviving our lives. Some of us have the good fortune to have a public arena to promote our personal dreams for the world. Others just barely hold on to their dreams. Dr. Susan Lawrence began in the smallest arena of all, her own internal world. One might say that she had no other choice, as her life wasn't working for her. Others will say that she has made a choice and has demonstrated the courage to take this time-consuming, expensive, often scary and painful lifelong journey of self-awareness. Maybe both are true. Whatever her initial conscious and unconscious motivations, we now get to see the payoff of her journey: a life of purpose, meaning, and clarity, as well as a wonderful new book.

Using both autobiography and biography, Susan gives us numerous examples of the consequences of unresolved grief and pain. Her stories show us how ineffective parenting leads both to socially acceptable and unacceptable dysfunction in the same family, from driven overachievement on the one hand to sociopathic and criminal behavior on the other.

In Susan's life story, we see the damage that may occur when parental and familial expectations for conformity overshadow the specific needs of a unique child. Susan feels an outcast and unlovable, imposing a self-exile as she leaves for college at a very young age. Determined to prove her own worthiness, she takes excessive risks to her physical body and, at the same time, commits to a career in cardiac surgery, one of medicine's most dramatic and esteemed fields. Life has other plans for Susan. When she experiences the poignancy of those facing death from cancer, she chooses oncology. However, even this path is a temporary way station on Susan's life journey. Simultaneously with her own self-exploration, Susan creates the Catalyst Foundation, initially for the treatment of other outcasts, those with HIV. Early on, there is a bit of rebelliousness and militancy to her work, born out of the self-righteousness that many of us carry from early neglect and injury.

We see that Susan does not wait until her own self-reclamation is complete. Rather, she commits herself to action, helping others as she tries to heal symbolically similar, internal wounds. As her own self-exploration progresses, Susan remains open to life's opportunities as one door closes. She progresses into HIV education and prevention for teenagers. When the school system rejects her work due to the explicit nature of its content, she opens another door, taking her program to the prisons.

My mentor, Elisabeth Kubler-Ross, used to teach that one of the universal laws is that "all true benefits are mutual." Susan confirms this law as she learns from those she seeks to help. She has the humility and introspection to see how her work in the world mirrors her internal world, initially driven by her pain but progressively motivated from her own healing and growth. Simultaneously, her work at the Catalyst Foundation begins a subtle shift from content-based care to process work.

In *Creating a Healing Society,* we witness a maturation and wisdom that comes not only from taking responsibility for and working through one's own unresolved grief but also from engaging in life's work. Gradually, Susan moves from her need to help the world's outcasts, those with Hermann Hesse's mark of Cain on their foreheads, to an understanding that underdogs and overlords have much in common. As Susan develops compassion for herself and works toward forgiveness for her family of origin, her militancy and rebelliousness drop away. Her purpose shifts from giving direct care to a specific group to providing an opportunity for healing in a larger system. With her own self-reclamation comes a new calmness, trust, and patience, as well as the courage to take her message to a broader audience.

In reading her stories, we become part of this audience. Susan's examples are beautifully written and build her case for a path to healing in our society. For those of us who are walking the same path, Susan is singing to the choir. But Susan has written her book as an invitation to others looking for an alternative in their lives and a roadmap for making a difference in the world. For "newcomers," I offer a few words of encouragement.

As you read, do not be put off by such harsh words as "abuse" and "neglect," especially if you are a parent. In her examples, Susan demonstrates with clarity how the "sins of the fathers (and mothers) are transmitted from generation to generation." These "sins" usually are the result of our own unresolved grief and pain, and often our attempts as parents to save our children from similar pain. These harsh words are not at all useful when they are spoken in condemnation of those who came before us. Nor are they meant to instill or increase paralyzing guilt in ourselves. Rather, they serve as a wake-up call for each of us to diagnose and explore how we were not seen and loved for who we are, and as the catalyst for breaking the cycle of generational dysfunction.

Susan's book is filled with stories of addiction, criminal behavior, and the disenfranchised of our society. Susan makes these stories real for all of us by writing simply and with clarity; it is therefore difficult to dismiss this book by saying, "I'm not like *them*." If you feel a visceral discomfort in reading this book, I urge you to begin the journey of exploring these uncomfortable feelings as your own, rather than projecting your fears outward onto *"those people."* I also urge you to notice the examples of everyday injuries caused by everyday moms and dads and teachers on everyday kids. These more subtle injuries, if internalized, produce the same feelings of fear, alienation, and unlovableness that perpetuate the cycle of disrespect, neglect, and violence that fills our world today.

Ultimately, this is a book about hope. Susan blesses us with redemptive stories of the most disenfranchised in our society. We witness how their capacity for introspection leads to understanding about the violent and self-destructive consequences of childhood abuse and neglect. We feel their true remorse for the suffering caused by projecting their pain onto the world rather than dealing with it themselves. Finally, we see them taking full responsibility for their current lives. A cycle is broken.

Where do we start to make a difference? I am uplifted by the possibilities for society as a whole because of one individual's personal journey of self-reclamation coupled with a life of meaningful work. I hope you are equally inspired by this wonderful little book.

Lawrence J. Lincoln, M.D.
Tucson, Arizona
June 2006

Introduction

Shortly before his death, my husband Sonny shared with me a profound observation. "I'm not dying of AIDS," he said. "I'm dying of the delayed effects of child abuse."

He delivered this simple remark in a calm and quiet voice, which magnified the enormity of its impact on me. For a moment, I felt as if I couldn't breathe. The truth of this statement, and its effect on my view of the world, was so intense that all I could do was remain present in silence.

Sonny's clear interpretation of his situation permanently transformed my understanding of the AIDS epidemic. My subsequent interactions with AIDS patients in my medical practice soon enabled me to see the truth of this concept as a universal principle. On the surface, my patients looked very different from one another; they were of diverse ethnicities, genders, cultural backgrounds, and socioeconomic levels. But their stories were connected by an underlying commonality: for each of them, unhealed trauma (from childhood abuse, neglect, or difficult life situations) unconsciously drove the risky behaviors which caused them to contract HIV.

At first, my awareness of the impact of human emotional pain and trauma on society was limited to the AIDS epidemic. Then, through my work with incarcerated teens, I learned the rest of the story. These young people, whose lives were consumed by gangs, violence, crime, and drugs, appeared to have nothing in common with adults living with AIDS. However, on a deep level, the same hidden process was playing out, although the teens unconsciously re-enacted the pain of their traumatic childhoods in different ways, and with different consequences to society. By expanding this thought process outward, I came to see that most, if not all, societal and world problems have unhealed human trauma as their root cause.

There is solid scientific evidence to support this somewhat intuitive viewpoint. In 1998, the Adverse Childhood Experiences (ACE) study, conducted by the Centers for Disease Control and Kaiser Permanente, was published in the American Journal of Preventive Medicine. The study involved nearly 10,000 Kaiser Permanente members who completed detailed questionnaires about seven categories of childhood trauma, referred to as ACE factors (physical, emotional, and sexual abuse; domestic violence; and household members who were substance abusers, mentally ill, or who had been incarcerated). One of the most important findings of this study is that childhood abuse is far more commonplace than we would like to believe. Among the mostly middle-class participants, half had been exposed to at least one ACE factor, a quarter to two factors, and a sixteenth to four or more; twenty two percent had been sexually abused as children. The study also powerfully illustrated the ongoing impact, often decades later, of traumatic childhood experiences on adult health. One astonishing finding was that boys with six or more categories of adverse childhood experiences were 4600% more likely than those with no ACE factors to use intravenous drugs later in life. Overall, for participants with four or more ACE categories, there was a four- to twelve-fold increased risk of alcoholism, drug abuse, depression, and suicide attempt; and a two- to four-fold increased risk of smoking, compulsive and unsafe sexual activity, and sexually transmitted disease. In the words of Dr. Vincent Felitti, co-principal investigator of the ACE study, "Adverse childhood experiences are the most important determinant of the health and well-being of our nation."

We are accustomed to thinking about the effects of childhood abuse on individuals; indeed, many of us know someone who grew up in traumatic circumstances and has difficulty as an adult with drug addiction, violence, eating disorders, or maintaining healthy relationships. Less clear for most of us are the consequences to society and the world when millions of wounded people are constantly engaging in these and other pain-driven behaviors. The consequences can be seen in the epidemics of AIDS, Hepatitis C, drug addiction, and alcoholism; in our violent and crime-ridden society; in unemployment, homelessness, and poverty; and, on an international level, in terrorism and war.

Our culture is often uncomfortable directly confronting the more distressing aspects of human existence, such as trauma, grief, and death. Through societal peer pressure, we are encouraged to "move on," "get over it," take prescription medications, or employ socially acceptable forms of distraction, such as materialism, television, video games, and superficial relationships. Unfortunately, these measures are simply not effective. Until we work through and gain power over our traumatic experiences, we are compelled, by the very nature of our humanity, to express our pain through the unconscious process of traumatic re-enactment, using the symbolic language of anti-social and self-destructive behaviors.

During the last century, Dr. Elisabeth Kubler-Ross transformed the way our culture deals with death. She taught that in order to die in peace, we must complete the "unfinished business" of our lives. Much of this "unfinished business" is the lingering effects of unhealed trauma. Through her work with dying patients, and through her writing, lectures, and workshops, Elisabeth helped a multitude of people face the end of their lives with clarity and courage, showing them how to work through their emotional pain and traumatic life experiences.

If we wish to live in a more peaceful and compassionate world, free of the devastation of widespread traumatic re-enactment, we must not wait until we are terminally ill to begin this process. Through an understanding of the universal human effects of trauma, and a commitment to our own personal growth and healing, we can reshape our society into one which eschews denial and escapism, and encourages and supports the working through of trauma as a normal part of human life.

I wrote this book because I believe these simple yet revolutionary concepts have the potential to change the world. I also believe the principles and strategies outlined will help anyone to become more healed, more balanced, and more of a force for good. I hope they also inspire you to become a leader in the creation of a healing society.

Himalayan Impression

Sometime in your life you will go on a journey.
It is the longest journey you have ever taken.
It is the journey to find yourself.

—Katherine Sharp

CHAPTER ONE

My Story:
The Subtle Nature of Trauma

Everything that was not suffered to the end and finally concluded,
recurred, and the same sorrows were undergone...
—Hermann Hesse, *Siddhartha*

When I was a small child, I had memories and feelings from another time. Whether this was actually another life, or a kind of pattern for my work in this one, I do not know. Whatever it was, this condition impacted me deeply, and it was something I kept secret from all but a very few people. I was born into a situation designed to recreate the emotional and spiritual work left unfinished from before. After a time, I came to see how the past constantly recurs in vast symbolic cycles, each one giving me the opportunity to examine and resolve things in ways which bring me increasing peace.

This life began in Brooklyn in the 1950's, when I was born to older parents who were surprised and overjoyed they could still have a child. My mother, Jeannette, had many secrets of her own: there were hints about her early life, such as that I had a much older half-brother who had been born when she was only fourteen. I knew she had been through a divorce (something quite uncommon for Jewish women in the 1940's) and her first husband had been abusive to the point of stalking her after she had left him. But my attempts to obtain more information were always met with great resistance: and so it was I learned there were things too horrible to be discussed and from which recovery was impossible.

My father, Alex, grew up in Poland during the First World War and married late in life; due, in part, to the responsibility he felt towards his parents. I knew more about his childhood than I did about my mother's, such as that he frequently had to hide in the basement from soldiers; and when he was about eight years old his parents, unable to support the entire family, sent him to live with a series of relatives who were less than enthusiastic about having him. My father told me he was chosen to go because he was the middle child, and therefore expendable: the older boy was needed to work and the younger one needed his mother. He maintained a stoic attitude about what must have been extremely frightening experiences, but expressed his pain through relationships in which he took care of other wounded individuals (such as my mother), unconsciously re-enacting his unhealed trauma. Only through this symbolic behavior was it evident how desperately he had wished to be safe, protected, and cared for as a child.

Like most people who are unconscious about the impact of trauma on their lives (and on their parenting abilities), my parents had no reservations about having a child, and in fact were delighted at the prospect of my birth. Perhaps they believed parenthood would render their difficult pasts inconsequential; or perhaps, like many people, they thought by sheer willpower alone they would refrain from passing on their unconscious legacy of abuse, abandonment, and war trauma. My parents surely had good intentions, and did not mean to hurt me; had I been a less complicated sort of child, one who grew into a less complicated sort of person, things might have turned out very differently.

But I required parents who would not be threatened by the individuality of their child, no matter how extreme. My parents' abandonment issues demanded that I fit into the family by being a traditional Jewish girl from Brooklyn; out of their own terror of loss, they did not welcome anything which deviated from this expectation. I was nothing like the child they must have envisioned.

I learned early on that within my family there were dire consequences to independent thought. In what may be my first memory, I am about two years old, standing next to our enormous black Buick sedan while my parents are getting ready to leave on a road trip. I don't want to go with them, and when my father opens the door for me to get in, I say a loud and firm "No!"

Perhaps this was the first time I had said "no" about anything, because I have the sense my father was shocked by my response. Without a word, he raised his hand and smacked me, hard, on the bottom. Sobbing piteously with pain, fear, and shame, I climbed into the car. In a most abrupt and violent manner, I had been made acutely aware of the danger of separateness.

My father, unconscious of the deeper message of this interaction, considered it a fine example of effective parenting. He would often relate the story with pride, ending it with, "After that, Susan never again refused to get into the car!" For me, however, this incident had a different meaning. It foreshadowed and crystallized one of the central issues in my life: the struggle to maintain my integrity in the face of suffocating pressure to conform.

This pressure was heightened by the influence of my father's extended family of four brothers and sisters-in-law, with whom my parents were very close: my Uncles Irving, Nat, Ike, and Sam, and their wives Aunts Edna, Claire, Sylvia, and Naomi. Perhaps because they had suffered greatly during the Holocaust, my extended family was very insular and viewed individuality as a form of betrayal. As a child I did not know what horrors were driving their attitudes and behaviors, and I did not understand that my way of being, so natural to me, was terrifying to them: I could only perceive that they considered me unacceptable the way I was. The frequent family gatherings I was forced to attend throughout my childhood were opportunities for my relatives to work on stamping out the alien parts of me. I felt helpless at these festivities, like a tiny bird being pecked to death by a horde of bigger ones.

This situation would have been far less destructive had my parents been able to protect me from my relatives' intrusive behavior and unkind words; but because of their own trauma-driven issues, they could not. During one family event, when I was about ten, my Uncle Irving said to me, "You shouldn't wear those clothes, Susan. They make you look too fat, and besides they don't match. You're getting older now and you should be more concerned about your appearance and your weight. You need to go on a diet." He reached over and pinched my stomach. "See that? That's where you need to lose the most weight."

Upon hearing this, I felt so hurt and ashamed I burst into tears on the spot, and ran away to find my parents. When I told them what my uncle had said, they responded, "Oh, you know how he is. He doesn't mean anything by it. Just forget it." When we left, my parents made me give Uncle Irving a hug and kiss, and tell him, "I love you." I felt intensely helpless, abandoned, and violated; it was sickening to be forced to feign affection for someone with whom I was so angry.

I cannot recall one circumstance in which my parents defended me to my extended family, or told them it was unacceptable to treat me in such ways. With few options to deal with this level of pain, I eventually banished from my consciousness most of my memories and feelings about specific interactions with my relatives, leaving me only with ill-defined impressions.

Beyond these routine instances of general invasiveness and insensitivity, my extended family had several particular issues with me. First, was the matter of my intellect: much to their dismay, I was unusually advanced academically. "Don't encourage it," my uncles and aunts advised my parents. "She won't be able to find a husband if she's too smart." Then, in total disregard of my family's rigidly held notions of gender roles, I was not at all interested in the usual things of concern to little girls, preferring instead the more active and rambunctious activities of little boys. "There must be something wrong with her," my relatives stated. "She's more like a boy than a girl. You should insist she wear dresses and makeup, and make her go to the dances at the Y." Finally, they informed my parents that I was a "cold fish," because I never wanted to hug or kiss any of them, and kept as much to myself as I could when I was made to visit their homes.

When I was small, I would tell my parents things I remembered which seemed to be from a time in the past. At first they listened indulgently, as adults do with highly imaginative children; but as I grew older and continued these discussions, they became increasingly worried about me. My parents were unable to envision any alternative explanations for my memories, and thus could only presume I was mentally ill. My relatives were especially uncomfortable with this situation; and while I am sure their motivations included genuine concern for my well-being, their intense reaction bespoke other, trauma-driven reasons. In paralyzed terror, I would sit at the dinner table during family gatherings and listen to my relatives, who were apparently oblivious to my presence, loudly advise my parents what they should do about me. Their position was I should be taken to a doctor and put on medication to eradicate my "abnormal" memories. To my parents' credit, they did not do so; but still I learned this aspect of myself was shameful and dangerous, and needed to be kept hidden at all costs. It was this, most of all, which made it impossible for me to be the child my family would have liked to have had.

When I was twelve years old I made a conscious decision that I would not, under any circumstances, surrender my integrity to my parents or my extended family. Like Andy Dufresne in *The Shawshank Redemption,* I devised a long-term plan of escape which enabled me to maintain my sanity. This involved using my intellectual abilities as my ticket to freedom: I would go to college at as young an age as possible, after which I would be liberated from my confinement and able to live the life of my choice.

My parents didn't really like it, and whenever I saw my relatives they were full of negativity about it, but I entered Barnard College when I was fourteen. While I had scholarships, took out student loans and worked part-time in the psychology lab, my parents still had to pay part of my tuition. Whenever I displeased them, I was reminded of the sacrifices being made so I could attend an Ivy League school; if I didn't behave myself, they would tell me, I would have to go to Brooklyn College. For the first three years at Barnard I had to live at home, but the two-hour subway ride each way into Manhattan was a time of freedom away from the pressing crush of my family.

Also when I was twelve, around the same time as I made my fateful commitment, I read about Christiaan Barnard, the South African surgeon who had performed the world's first human heart transplant. I was fascinated by his miraculous achievement, and felt drawn to him as a person. I wrote to him, and to my amazement he wrote back; we soon became pen pals, he serving as my long-distance mentor. He inspired me to go to medical school to become a heart surgeon, to have a life full of thrilling accomplishments, as he had done. Through Dr. Barnard, I met Dr. Denton Cooley, another famous heart surgeon at the Texas Heart Institute in Houston. During my last two summer vacations from college, I went there by myself to spend time in the operating room with Dr. Cooley and his team.

When I was seventeen, I was accepted by Baylor College of Medicine. I was ecstatic: not only was I on the path towards what I saw as a brilliant career, but I had also succeeded in putting two thousand miles between myself and my family. And all of this in five years! On the surface, it seemed as though I had freed myself from the constraints of my childhood. My family had not been successful in breaking my will and molding me to their expectations. I had won.

But not quite. There was something sinister and uncontrollable within me, which in time came to dominate my life. I first became aware of it when I was about twelve, as I was getting off the bus with my mother at our stop on Nostrand Avenue in Brooklyn. At the moment I stepped down to the curb, I felt the most peculiar sensation in the pit of my stomach: not nausea exactly, and not pain, but a kind of highly unpleasant churning.

"My stomach feels really weird," I called out to my mother, who had gotten off the bus ahead of me. "I think I'm getting sick."

I don't remember what my mother said, or anything else about that episode, either. However, the revolting feeling returned with increasing frequency: often when I was distressed emotionally, but just as often for no apparent reason. Soon I realized I was actually feeling depressed, and the disgusting stomach sensation was a physical manifestation of depression. The problem was disabling at times, and no matter how hard I struggled against it, I could not control it, even by the not-inconsiderable power of my will. Even today I am mystified at how I was able to complete my education in the face of such unrelenting turmoil.

While education appeared, superficially, to be the main focus of my life, by the time I had graduated from college there remained the deeper, more urgent matter: to discover the truth of myself and why, despite my external achievements, I lived in complete and utter misery. Casual social interactions were difficult for me, close friendships even more so, and intimate relationships impossible; I had a horror of physical touch, and was equally terrified of emotional invasion. The only time I felt safe in relating to people was when I was in the role of doctor; in my private life my closest companions were animals, especially my cats.

For years, I sought help from psychiatrists and psychotherapists; I wrote my feelings out in voluminous journals; and I read the works of great writers of the past who had suffered similarly. (Hermann Hesse was my particular favorite. I loved these words from *Demian,* which stated so poignantly the central theme of my life: "All I wanted was to live in accord with the promptings which came from my true self. Why was that so very difficult?") However, despite all of my efforts, I made no progress with any of it. My despair worsened as I came to believe it was my fault I was this way, and that it was incurable.

For the first three years of medical school, despite the personal issues with which I struggled, I remained dedicated to the goal of becoming a heart surgeon. I kept up my correspondence with Dr. Barnard, and still spent time visiting with Dr. Cooley. Then, I took a one-month rotation in medical oncology, and found myself drawn to working with the terminally ill. For reasons which were at that time unclear to me, I was very comfortable talking honestly with people about death, something most dying people need and greatly appreciate. After graduation from medical school, rather than seeking a surgical residency as I had always planned, I began my training in internal medicine.

Once again, I managed to submerge my personal torment sufficiently to get through five more years of study (internship, residency, and fellowship) in order to become a board-certified medical oncologist. When I was done, I needed to find a job. It didn't matter, really, where I went: I had no ties with anyone, and I was, quite honestly, too exhausted from the constant struggle with depression and old memories to care. I saw an ad in the *Journal of the American Medical Association* for a medical oncology position in the Antelope Valley, a Southern California desert community sixty miles north of Los Angeles. I went there for an interview and it seemed satisfactory: if nothing else, I thought, I could now be as far away from my family as possible while still remaining on the same continent.

* * *

I established my private practice of medical oncology in Lancaster, at that time the largest city in the Antelope Valley, which I soon found out was a mostly very conservative community with a vocal fundamentalist Christian base. There was a competing oncology group in town whose philosophy was very different than mine: they rarely referred patients to a hospice program, but instead encouraged them to continue chemotherapy and radiation treatments until the very end of their lives. Cancer patients who wanted a different approach came to my office. As word spread that I was a doctor who would have honest yet compassionate discussions with dying people and their families, I became very busy.

It was the mid-eighties, the early years of the AIDS epidemic. Lancaster was close enough to Los Angeles, one of the major metropolitan areas most impacted by AIDS, to have a significant number of residents living with HIV. My training as a medical oncologist had made me quite comfortable in treating AIDS; it was, in those days, a terminal illness, and many of the drugs used in its treatment were similar to those I prescribed for cancer chemotherapy. I welcomed people with AIDS into my practice, to the consternation of many elements of our conservative community. The reaction of most of my fellow doctors was one of relief, however, because they were definitely not interested in treating these patients. I soon became known as the Antelope Valley's AIDS specialist, and when doctors in our community came across people with HIV in their practices, they would hand them a referral slip which read, "See Dr. Susan Lawrence."

After several months, I was asked to become the volunteer Medical Director of the local hospice, which was an in-home program operated by the Visiting Nurse Association. My duties included attending weekly meetings of the hospice staff, giving advice on pain management, and making home visits to terminally ill patients whose own physicians would not do so. The position also gave me the opportunity to educate the community about death and dying issues, as well as the need for compassion and respect for people with AIDS.

On the surface, it seemed things were going well for me in my new life. It had always been the case, however, that whenever I moved to a new city, I usually experienced a brief respite from my personal anguish. Lancaster was no exception. Once I had gotten used to life there, the same pattern emerged. After so many years, it was now increasingly difficult to function in the outside world as I became more and more drained from the effort of dealing with the agony of my inner world. I felt I must be nearing the end of this struggle, coming closer to the time in which I would, at best, be confined to a mental hospital; or, at worst, commit suicide.

But until that time came, I was still desperate for help. Although I had tried therapy many times before without success, I was willing to try again. I felt sufficiently comfortable with the Nursing Director at the hospice to ask her for a referral. Without hesitation, she wrote down one name and phone number on a piece of paper and handed it to me.

* * *

When I first went to see Sharon, the therapist who saved my life and enabled me to use my talents, I told her I was just too weak to deal with the circumstances of my existence. I had always heard from my parents and extended family that I was the one with the problem; and indeed, this appeared to be true. They all seemed to fit comfortably into the lives they had been given. I never heard that any of them had unexplainable memories, appeared to be the wrong gender, possessed freakish intelligence, or any of the other features of my existence which seemed to trouble them so much. It had never once occurred to me I was not the one with the problem.

From Sharon I began to learn about the nature and meaning of childhood abuse and other life traumas; gradually, I came to see that my suffering was from the continuing impact of some very painful situations, which had been created by people who were themselves in pain. The end to my anguish lay in recovery from these aftereffects.

The process of recovery was long and difficult. I made it a priority, working only part-time at my medical practice. I went to individual and group therapy several times each week, and attended many week-long residential workshops for survivors of abuse and trauma. I took trips to places of significance for me from my past, to come to terms with things that had happened there. Perhaps most importantly, I gained an understanding of my own personal spirituality. I came to rely on guidance and support from the "Other Side," by which I mean my connection with God, the universe, and those who have passed on. Even with all of this, it took three years before there was any difference in how I felt; until one day I noticed, almost in passing, I was no longer living in daily torment.

It was around this time I met Sonny.

Touchstones

Love takes off the masks we fear we cannot live without
and know we cannot live within.

—James Baldwin

CHAPTER TWO

Sonny:
Trauma and AIDS

*We can choose to see AIDS as a grim crisis for humanity or as
an extraordinary opportunity, individually and collectively,
to move forward.*
—Christopher Spence

Ten years older and rougher around the edges, Sonny Bartz and I had little in common, outwardly. Deeper, we shared many connections, both mundane and profound; he grew up in the nearby New York borough of Queens, and also ended up in the same dusty slice of Southern California. Synchronicity works to connect those whose lives need to mesh.

Sonny's childhood was, for the most part, one of continual abandonment and helplessness. The only boy among three sisters, Sonny was expected to fend for himself; his mother (for unclear but certainly trauma-based reasons of her own) felt her daughters, more so than her son, needed her attention and support. There was violence in Sonny's home, often related to his father's problem with alcohol. One of his most terrifying memories as a small child was when he witnessed his father threatening to stab his pregnant mother in the abdomen with a large kitchen knife. Sonny was also often the target of his father's violence; however, as he had no other frame of reference as a child, he accepted such things as unpleasant but normal. In stark contrast to these difficulties, Sonny delighted in the fact that his parents chose his nickname (his real name was Milton) because, as he put it, he was "the sunshine of their lives." This, and other positive features of his childhood, interspersed as they were between episodes of fear and horror, enabled Sonny to feel (as is usual in trauma-bonding) close and connected to his family despite the pain they caused him.

Sonny's unconscious flight from his childhood grief began as a teenager, when he formed a gang (the "Alley Cats") with some similarly affected boys from his neighborhood. Being a member of this gang, and his individual friendships with these boys, was extremely important to him because it was the only area of his life in which he didn't feel abandoned or helpless. With his friends, Sonny began drinking, using drugs, and taking part in anti-social activities such as vandalism and stealing cars. Sadly, his family (and others around him who might have been able to help) could not interpret the symbolic language of this behavior, trapped as they were by their own trauma-driven attitudes and perceptions.

When Sonny was fourteen, his father was hospitalized for several days and then died suddenly of a heart attack. This loss brought to the surface extremely difficult and confusing emotions for Sonny, whose feelings for his father were ambivalent and complex. This was compounded by terrible guilt, as he didn't visit his father in the hospital before he died, so absorbed was he in the pain-avoidance of gang life. With no assistance in working through these feelings, Sonny became even more deeply involved with drugs, alcohol, and crime. By the time he was seventeen, he was injecting heroin.

This downward spiral of traumatic re-enactment was interrupted when Sonny abruptly decided to join the Navy. His mother, still very much involved in the lives of her daughters, had no idea how to help him and was glad to give her permission for him to enlist. After a rocky start, Sonny thrived in the Navy; his commanding officer was able to see that beneath the angry, tough-guy façade was a likeable, bright, and capable young man who was in a great deal of pain. He encouraged Sonny, and treated him with respect and compassion, while setting clear limits on his behavior. At the end of four years of service, Sonny seriously considered making the Navy his career.

But like so many people who have not resolved trauma-related family issues, he felt drawn to return home. He unconsciously yearned for a magical transformation of his toxic relationship with his family into one of loving connection, and he went back to seek exactly this kind of resolution.

The Antelope Valley, where Sonny's family had relocated to take advantage of the job opportunities within the aerospace industry, is one of the methamphetamine capitals of California. It was not long after his reunion with his family, and its inevitable disappointment, that Sonny tried speed for the first time; very quickly the drug took over his life, erasing much of the progress he had made during the four years in the Navy. He was deeply ashamed that he was an IV drug user, or "lowlife hype" as he referred to himself; but his shame was not enough to put a stop to his self-destruction. Despite arrests and jail time, somehow Sonny was able to function as an aircraft mechanic at Lockheed. Even so, the drug had transformed him into a violent, cruel, selfish person who seemingly had no conscience: a person who could never be vulnerable enough to recognize that through his actions he spoke the symbolic language of his childhood pain.

In 1985, while he was still working at Lockheed, Sonny nearly died of a drug overdose during a weekend of partying. This experience terrified him, and his desperation enabled him to put aside his shame that he was an IV drug addict. He went to his boss at Lockheed, rolled up his sleeves to show his bruised and damaged veins, and began sobbing for help. The next day he entered the Care Unit, an inpatient drug rehab program.

* * *

Sonny loved his new life as a clean and sober man. During the next three years, he continuously worked to transform himself into a person he was proud to be: the person he perhaps always could have been had he received help in working through his childhood abuse and trauma. He conducted himself with honesty and integrity, taking great pride in his work at Lockheed, and gaining recognition as an outstanding employee. Due to his exceptional ability to relate to people, he was elected Union Steward. He learned new ways of dealing with emotional pain, so he no longer needed to use drugs or violence as a way to avoid feelings of helplessness or abandonment. He had an outrageous sense of humor, which he used effectively to defuse uncomfortable situations. He was also so compassionate and caring that when he had to talk with a co-worker about body odor (one of his Union Steward tasks) the man left the conversation smiling and not in the least embarrassed.

He grew into being a profoundly spiritual man, with a deep connection to God and the Other Side. It was this connection, more than anything else, that sustained him in what was to come.

During Sonny's stay in the Care Unit, the HIV test had only been available for a few months. Because of his long history of sharing drug needles, the staff suggested to Sonny that he be tested, and he agreed. He was overjoyed when he was told his test was negative, that he had not contracted HIV. Sonny believed God had something special in mind for him to have spared his life, and this further motivated him to continue his personal and spiritual growth work.

Sonny had been clean and sober for three years when he became ill with what he thought was a bad case of the flu. Persistent high fevers and shortness of breath finally forced him to see a doctor, who did a chest X-ray and immediately admitted him to the hospital. Further testing revealed that he had pneumonia caused by the fungus Pneumocystis carinii, a common AIDS-defining infection. Sonny was devastated, even more so because no one at the hospital would talk with him about his condition. When he was discharged, he was handed one of those referral slips: "See Dr. Susan Lawrence."

A few weeks later, I met Sonny. He was sitting in one of the exam rooms in my office, desolately holding his head in his hands. As I walked in, he looked up at me with a flickering hope burning in his eyes; he was still praying for the AIDS diagnosis to be a mistake. After all, he told me earnestly, he hadn't put himself at risk even once since the negative test in the Care Unit.

I had already reviewed his medical records, and knew the mistake lay in the Care Unit's interpretation of Sonny's HIV test results. The HIV antibody test had been positive, but the Western Blot test, done to confirm a positive antibody test, was "indeterminate." Apparently, this was the reason that Sonny was told he did not have HIV. When he had been re-tested during his treatment for Pneumocystis, both the antibody and Western Blot tests had been positive. As gently as I could, I told Sonny the truth: he had already been infected with HIV before he stopped using drugs.

"While it is true that you have AIDS," I went on, "we are going to work together to ensure that you live as long as possible and have the best quality of life you can. There is always hope; so much research is going on, and a major breakthrough in treatment could occur at any time."

Sonny seemed much calmer than he did at the beginning of the visit. We talked about preventive treatments for Pneumocystis, starting AZT (the only drug available in 1988), and doing more blood work. Sonny made a follow-up appointment and left. Neither of us could have anticipated how radically that meeting would change the rest of our lives.

* * *

Sonny would come to see me for follow-up visits every few weeks. After the medical discussion was over, he would usually talk to me about various aspects of his life. The conversation invariably returned, however, to the subjects of redemption, death, and the meaning of life: matters with which I felt a deep resonance. I remember one conversation in which Sonny wondered if there could ever be any redeeming value to the life of an ex-hype with AIDS. I had come to respect and admire him so much that I immediately responded, "I can see enormous value in such a life: and I wouldn't even put the word 'redeeming' with it." Sonny looked at me with a stunned expression, as though he could not imagine anyone would ever say something like that about him. I could tell this had impacted him greatly.

Over a year passed, during which Sonny and I became good friends, although within the confines of my office. I admired his quick wit and fantastic sense of humor, his introspective ability and his spiritual connection; the way he intuitively understood people; and most of all his courage in allowing himself to be vulnerable in the face of his certain death. For his part, Sonny's relationship with me enabled him to imagine the possibility that he might actually be worth more than just the worst mistake of his life.

Finally, we decided to become friends outside of the office, and began doing things such as eating out in restaurants, going to the movies and to the zoo. It was during this time I began to learn, through Sonny's example, how to live in the world. I would observe Sonny relating with people in social situations I previously would have completely avoided, and was astonished to see that most people are not unbearably intrusive (as my family had been). Through practice, and with Sonny's help, I learned I could feel safe when interacting with people. It was, for me, an unimaginable achievement.

I greatly admired Sonny's ability to work through difficult situations and painful feelings to come to a healthy resolution. When we visited the Antelope Valley Fair, Sonny met one of his co-workers from Lockheed and began a conversation with him. While they were talking, I left to buy some food; when I returned, Sonny was standing by himself, looking extremely shaken and upset. He didn't want to tell me what had happened, and was very quiet for the remainder of our time together.

For most of the next week, it was obvious that Sonny was processing something very painful. He declined my invitations to go out and told me he needed to be alone. After many days, he shared with me what was going on.

When Sonny first returned to work at Lockheed after recovering from Pneumocystis pneumonia, there were rumors that he had AIDS. He had decided he was going to keep his medical condition private; he remembered the cruel comments that had been made a few years before when a co-worker had died of AIDS. The group hadn't even wanted to send flowers to the man's funeral.

Sonny was shocked and deeply hurt to hear the following comment from his co-worker during their casual conversation at the Fair: "Hey, man, I heard you have AIDS. I didn't know you took it in the ass!"

"At first," Sonny told me, "I just wanted to go to the guy's house with a gun and blow his brains out. What could they do to me? Put me in jail? I have AIDS. I'm going to die anyway, so who cares?

"I obsessed about that for two days. Then, I realized blowing the guy's brains out really wasn't in my best interest. I don't want to die in prison, where nobody gives a shit about you. Since I have to die, I want as much control as possible over how and where that happens. I'm not going to let some idiot take that away from me.

"Finally," he went on, "I understood that the only thing I can do is have compassion for the guy, because he's not capable of anything more than being cruel to a dying man."

This last statement took my breath away with its truth and power. I just stared at Sonny in amazement.

A few weeks later, when we were eating dinner in a restaurant, this same co-worker came in and was seated a few tables away from us. When we got up to leave, Sonny went over to him and said with a smile, "Hey, man. How are you doing? Good to see you." It was an inspirational lesson for me in dignity and compassion; one which I constantly (but not always successfully) strive to emulate.

Several more months passed; Sonny and I came to see we were not only best friends, but that we loved each other. This prompted a search for a new doctor to take over Sonny's medical care. We interviewed several AIDS specialists in Los Angeles, but were not comfortable with any of them. Finally, we arranged with a caring family practitioner in Lancaster to become Sonny's primary doctor, with the understanding that he would consult with me about AIDS treatment.

By the time Sonny and I married on March 21, 1992, he had been living with AIDS for nearly four years. The disease had begun to take its toll. No longer able to work, he was on disability-retirement from Lockheed, and so weak he needed a caregiver to stay with him when he was home alone. Yet, we were content. We knew from the outset our time together would be limited, and were at peace with that. We were immensely grateful for the gifts of transformation each had brought to the other's life.

In the year prior to his death, Sonny and I began work on The Catalyst Foundation. We chose the name in recognition that, rather than becoming an AIDS "victim," Sonny used his life with AIDS as a catalyst for personal and spiritual growth. Catalyst became a nonprofit organization with a founding mission to provide medical care and supportive services to people with HIV/AIDS in our small, conservative community. Sonny felt fortunate he had been able to provide for his needs through good health insurance, savings, and a pension from Lockheed; but he knew many other people with AIDS were not so lucky. He not only wanted to leave something behind for others in need, but he also wanted to create a mechanism for educating the community about the importance of compassion and respect for all people, including those with AIDS. He launched this project, as well as Catalyst's HIV prevention program, by speaking about his life and his struggle with AIDS to a group of middle school students in Lancaster.

His work done, Sonny died peacefully at home on July 25, 1993. My bereavement was nothing like I had expected; rather than the crushing grief I had instinctively assumed I would experience, I instead felt powerfully connected to Sonny. It was as though, in the weeks and months leading up to his death, he and I were preparing, each in our own way, for a very natural and even beautiful transition. Our relationship continued despite his physical invisibility, with synchronistic happenstances becoming (and remaining to this day) our form of communication. Two weeks after his passing, I closed my medical practice and The Catalyst Foundation officially opened its doors: an event in which I knew Sonny participated from his special vantage point on the Other Side.

* * *

My relationship with Sonny forever altered my view of the world. His brilliant observation that he was not dying of AIDS, but of the delayed effects of child abuse, was the beginning of my understanding that human emotional pain, abuse, and trauma are the major underlying causes of the most serious problems that face our society and our world today. At first, I saw this only as it applied to the AIDS epidemic; but my awareness was soon to be greatly expanded through my work at Catalyst with incarcerated teens, and through the wisdom and insight of another extraordinary man.

The Middle Passage

*What lies behind us and what lies before us are small matters
compared to what lies within us.*

—Ralph Waldo Emerson

CHAPTER THREE

Frank:
Trauma as the Driving Force
of Societal Ills

Life shrinks or expands in proportion to one's courage.
—Anais Nin, *The Diary of Anais Nin, volume 3, 1939–1944*

Frank Altadonna grew up in Brooklyn during the Sixties in a cold and distant Italian family. His childhood circumstances were, not surprisingly, nearly identical to Sonny's, in ways both obvious and subtle. The only boy among three sisters, Frankie (as he was then called) was left from a young age to look after himself. As in Sonny's family, Frank's mother was also of the belief that boys didn't need the care, support, and supervision girls did; therefore, she, too, focused her parenting energies primarily on her daughters. Frank's father, who worked long hours in construction, came home tired and didn't have the time or energy to connect emotionally with his young son; besides, from the outset, he hadn't been thrilled with the idea of having children anyway.

As far back as he could remember, it was always of great importance to Frank that he be able to support himself financially. By the age of nine, he was already employed with a paper route; he also did jobs for his neighbors, such as shoveling snow from their driveways in the winter. When he was fourteen he began working after school and on weekends at a dry cleaners. On the surface it looked like Frank was an enterprising, self-motivated boy who was destined for a successful career in business; but lurking at the edge of his consciousness was the awareness that he could expect no help from his family so he had better take care of himself. It was only in the year prior to his death he came to understand the fear and grief of the abandoned little boy which drove this need.

Having little parental supervision, Frank ran the streets of Brooklyn from a very young age, usually with older kids. It was the Sixties, drugs were plentiful, and there was no one to offer him more positive activities. At the age of nine Frank began experimenting with drugs: sniffing glue, drinking, smoking pot, and taking pills. There was so little mind paid to him at home that no one suspected what he was doing, especially since he kept his grades up at school, always had a job, and avoided attracting negative attention from teachers.

Years later, when Frank and I were becoming friends (and he was just beginning to be aware that childhood neglect had deeply impacted his life), I asked him what had been going on that he began using drugs at such a young age. At first, he replied in an offhand way, "Oh, I was a cool kid, and I was just having fun." Several weeks later, however, he told me seriously, "I thought a lot about your question. I think I used drugs because I needed to change the way I felt." When I asked him what he had been feeling that needed to be changed, he responded, "I just didn't want to feel like myself, even if it was good."

Frank's drug use escalated as he got older. When he was thirteen, a pivotal incident occurred which demonstrated to him clearly that his parents were not able or willing to intervene no matter how obvious his drug use. It set the stage for the unconscious, pain-driven choices Frank subsequently made which ultimately led to his death.

Always the introspective, Frank began taking LSD in his early teens, which he believed enhanced his ability to study himself. On one occasion, the effects of the drug persisted, and were severe enough for his parents to notice; Frank appeared confused, and had difficulty walking and speaking. After several days without improvement, his parents took him to the emergency room, where he was admitted to the hospital for observation. He remained there for a week.

When Frank's symptoms resolved and he was ready to be discharged, the doctor had a conference with him and his parents. "You need to know," the doctor told Frank's parents, "your son has been taking LSD. That's why he had this psychotic reaction."

Frank's parents looked at each other and said nothing. Frank, terrified, assumed he was in big trouble. On the way home from the hospital, there was total silence in the car, during which he imagined his parents were planning, each in their own mind, a major consequence for him which would be revealed once they were in the privacy of their house. But he was shocked by what actually happened, which was ... nothing.

Not a word was ever said to him by either of his parents about his use of LSD or about his week in the hospital. Perhaps they felt that the hospital stay was enough of a consequence to make Frank quit using drugs; or perhaps they just didn't know how to even begin to deal with the situation. In any case, one message Frank got from this (which his teenage self liked in a surface way) was he could do as he pleased and his parents were not going to get involved. However, although unaware of it at the time, he also grieved that his parents didn't consider him important enough to expend their time and energy, even to put aside their own pain and fear, to stop his self-destruction.

During the summer before his senior year of high school, Frank was offered an opportunity to make money by selling drugs. At first, he declined; Frank had an especially well-developed conscience ("It enters the room before I do," he used to say) and he didn't want to be a drug dealer. However, he was slowly and imperceptibly drawn into these activities when he saw how much money his friends were making and how easy it was. What allowed him to override his conscience was the powerful yet unconscious drive to be independent in all ways from his family. Frank never wanted to be in the position of needing to ask his family for money (or anything else, for that matter) because this presented the possibility he might become painfully aware of the full extent of his abandonment.

Frank told himself he would sell drugs "just for the summer," but within two months he had made $15,000 on an initial investment of $500. He was hooked.

* * *

Frank's life as a drug dealer was agonizing. He tried his best to maintain an outward sense of normality; he graduated from high school, found a job at a local bank, and took classes at the community college. But his deepest concern was the dilemma from which he was unable to extricate himself. He was tortured by his conscience over his drug dealing, yet he was prevented from stopping by an excruciating form of emotional paralysis centered around his fear of needing assistance from his family. Frank dealt with this in the only way he knew: by using more and harder drugs to disable his conscience and eradicate his anguish. Before long he was addicted to heroin.

Still not able to address directly his heroin addiction or his drug dealing, Frank's unconscious finally took action, and he set about sabotaging his drug business. Frank had been known as "the honest drug dealer" (this oxymoron being the remarkable by-product of his determined conscience), because his customers could always count on him to show up and never cheat them; as a result, he was highly successful and made a lot of money. But now he began missing appointments for deals, as his own drug use escalated dramatically; the trappings of his "normal" life fell away as he lost his bank job and dropped out of his college classes.

During that year, in desperation, Frank turned to his parents (one of the very few times in his life he did so). Frank's family had (like Sonny's) left New York for the Antelope Valley for the employment opportunities there. He begged them on the phone to help him come out to California to stay with them, where he could get away from the drug business and start over. They refused, but told him they were planning a trip to New York to visit friends the following year; he could go back with them then, if that's what he still wanted to do. By the time they arrived, Frank was broke, homeless, and sleeping in Brooklyn's Prospect Park.

* * *

Frank got high one last time, just before boarding the plane to Los Angeles. Then he shut the door on his old life, insofar as was possible with the hidden yet dominating effects of his childhood following him.

Within three days, he had a job at Wickes Lumber. Instead of the $3,000 a week he was making as a drug dealer, he would now be earning $3.80 an hour; but he was so grateful to be at peace with his conscience that he couldn't care less. Miraculously, he was able to quit heroin with no withdrawal symptoms whatsoever: a testament to the strength of his will and his powers of dissociation. It wasn't long before he found a job with higher pay in Housing Maintenance at Edwards Air Force Base, where he would work for the next eight years. He was able to move out of his parents' house and begin his own life, this time free of drugs.

Five years passed, during which Frank lived a quiet life as a carpenter-mason. In 1987, he began to notice seemingly minor changes in his health, such as recurrent sinus infections. Concerned about the frequency with which Frank needed antibiotics for these infections, his doctor decided to investigate further. When all the tests came back normal (including a bone marrow test to look into the reason for an elevated protein level in his blood), the doctor informed him he could find nothing seriously wrong.

As Frank would later relate, he then hesitantly told his doctor about his past as a heroin addict. "I shared needles a few times, but I don't think it was enough for me to get anything," he said. "Still, maybe I should get tested for HIV?"

Two weeks later, Frank learned his test was positive, and his doctor told him he had two years to live. He was devastated and very depressed; he even considered suicide, which he felt was better than becoming debilitated from AIDS and having to once again turn to his family for support. Gradually, though, he came to realize his doctor's prediction for his survival was inaccurate; aside from the sinus infections his health was actually quite good. For the next five years, he simply went on with his life, often feeling as though nothing had changed.

But, in time, illness due to HIV became all-consuming for Frank. When he first came to The Catalyst Foundation in 1994, his health had already begun to deteriorate. He had been unable to work for the past two years due to HIV-related nerve damage in his legs, a painful condition called peripheral neuropathy. And he had recently been diagnosed with Hepatitis C, which he had also contracted through sharing needles so long ago. Frank was lonely and missed working; he wanted to see if Catalyst might need a volunteer.

At that time I was in the process of starting our HIV prevention program for incarcerated teens, and was just beginning to do classroom presentations for the boys at Challenger Memorial Youth Center, a youth probation camp located not far from the Catalyst office. I would start by telling Sonny's story, which always got the boys' attention, and then teach them about HIV/AIDS and how they could prevent themselves from becoming infected. Frank came out to Challenger with me to see the program, and he loved it. It was the beginning of an extraordinary collaboration.

Frank soon became Catalyst's first HIV Prevention Program Coordinator. He learned to share his story with the boys in the camp, and recruited and trained other people with HIV to become speakers for the program. Not only was he responsible for the oversight and development of the Challenger program, but he also expanded Catalyst's HIV prevention activities to areas outside our small community. Frank had an amazing work ethic, which was all the more remarkable because he was, by this time, a very sick man. He was also devoted to Catalyst, in part because it permitted him to use his difficult past to be of service to others, rather than hiding the truth of himself in shame.

By 1997, Frank and I were teaching three classes a week at Challenger. After one class, a boy came up to us and said, "I've heard your program ten times, and I know all the information now about HIV prevention. Can you let me help you teach?"

Frank and I knew this was a great idea, and the Challenger administration liked it, too. Within a few months Catalyst's HIV Peer Educator training program was initiated, with Ernest D., the boy who made the suggestion, taking a leadership role in the first graduating class. Now, at each classroom presentation, peer educators taught the HIV prevention information; and Frank and I were at Challenger an additional two days a week, facilitating peer educator training sessions.

It was my work with the boys in the peer educator program which enabled me to see that the impact of human emotional pain, abuse, and trauma was not limited to AIDS, but was, in fact, the driving force underlying our most serious societal problems, including gangs, drugs, violence, crime, and the ongoing cycle of child abuse. Challenger is a locked facility, and many of the boys sent there had committed violent crimes; the vast majority were gang members and drug users. As they shared with me about their lives, their families, and their childhoods, I could see that although the stories sounded different on the surface, the same basic factors were operating underneath. The boys felt an overwhelming helplessness and sense of abandonment, often caused by parents who had suffered through their own traumatic and abusive childhoods; parents who were not able to work through these issues and their long-term effects sufficiently to stop the cycle, to break the chain of transmission from generation to generation.

Frank and I often discussed these issues, which we called "the mission." We believed any effort to address society's problems would not be successful without an understanding of the impact of trauma on human beings. It became Catalyst's mission to raise public awareness of this concept.

We had been working together for four years, and had become very close; I trusted and respected Frank greatly and considered him my best friend. Frank was concerned with deep spiritual matters (which also contained great meaning for me), and he had an incredible ability to do significant work on his childhood abuse and neglect issues, often through dreams. Once, after a particularly amazing conversation, I told him, "You're more like Sonny than anyone I ever met," at which Frank just smiled to himself.

Of course, we loved each other; it just took us some time to get to the point of being able to say it out loud. Finally, in March of 1998, we did; this added dimension to our friendship greatly enriched our lives. A few months later, someone at Challenger took pictures of the staff along with the current class of peer educator graduates. Frank stood proudly with the group, a huge smile of delight replacing his usually serious expression. "Oh my God, Frank," I exclaimed when I saw the pictures. "It shows in your face!"

* * *

By this time, many advances had been made in the treatment of HIV; new highly effective medications were available, and HIV was no longer an automatic death sentence. Frank was taking some of these new medications, and his HIV was under control; however, he was becoming increasingly ill from progressive liver disease due to

Hepatitis C. His doctor, Dale Prokupek, a specialist in the treatment of Hepatitis C, was concerned about Frank's liver, especially when he had been unable to tolerate a course of interferon, the only treatment available at the time. Frank had also had an episode of severe liver failure, from which he had miraculously recovered; still, things did not look good.

In the summer of 1998, I went with Frank to one of his medical appointments. After he had finished his examination and review of Frank's blood tests, Dr. Prokupek sat down in the exam room to tell us something astounding. There was a research study being done at the University of Pittsburgh Medical Center on liver transplantation for people with HIV; would Frank consider going there to be evaluated for a liver transplant?

Until that moment, we had never even imagined the possibility of a liver transplant, as people with HIV had always been ineligible for such procedures. AIDS was considered a terminal illness, so transplant programs did not want to use an organ for someone whose life expectancy was so limited; plus, the immunosuppressive drugs required after transplant surgery would drastically weaken the immune system of someone with HIV. Dr. Prokupek explained to us the success of the new HIV medications had changed all that.

Frank betrayed no emotion during this discussion, while I was so shocked as to be almost speechless. He told Dr. Prokupek he would think about it and get back to him.

Frank spent the next three months making his decision. While I wondered what could be taking him so long, and frequently wanted to scream at him, "Why don't we go to Pittsburgh now?!," he was resolving important personal issues from his past. Frank knew if he decided to seek a transplant, his family would do nothing to help, which would bring up tremendously painful feelings of abandonment. This was the issue he had spent his entire life avoiding through the oblivion of drugs; it was, in fact, the root cause of his being in need of a liver transplant in the first place. He was now struggling to see if he could bear to face up to it.

Finally, Frank reached his decision. "I have given my family power over me long enough," he told me. "I want to live, and I am going to Pittsburgh."

True to Frank's prediction, his family stood by and did nothing; it was astonishing for me to witness how cold and uncaring they seemed. Frank's insurance would not cover the full cost of the operation, so we began working with the National Foundation for Transplants to help us raise additional funds. We formed a volunteer group, the Friends of Frank Altadonna Liver Transplant Fundraising Team, and a representative from the Foundation came to our first meeting to help us get organized. There was a large turnout for this meeting, including our co-workers at Catalyst, staff members from Challenger, and people from the community who knew of Frank and his work: but no one from Frank's family. As he watched the room fill up with people who had come there for no other reason than they cared about him, Frank was overcome with emotion. He put his head down on the table and sobbed. It was, for him, an enormously healing moment.

* * *

For the next five months, when we weren't working at Catalyst or with the teens at Challenger, Frank and I dedicated ourselves to making a reality our dream of a successful liver transplant. In October 1998 we traveled to the University of Pittsburgh Medical Center for an intensive week-long evaluation, which would qualify Frank to be placed on the transplant waiting list.

Although he knew it was his only hope, the idea of this surgery terrified Frank. He prayed that when the time came for the transplant, he would be so sick as to be comatose, and thus not be aware he was about to be anesthetized for perhaps the last time. During the evaluation, it was this fear which prompted Frank to ask one of the surgeons when the optimal time for his liver transplant would be; he was greatly unnerved by the answer.

"I would operate right now if we had a liver for you," said the doctor, in a direct but not unkind manner. "The average life expectancy with your stage of liver disease is about six months, but the waiting list for a liver of your blood type is two years long."

While Frank sat, absorbing this information in stunned silence, I was determined not to leave without extracting some sort of hope from this meeting. "But isn't it true the sickest person gets moved to the top of the list, no matter how long they have been on it?" I asked.

"That is so," the surgeon replied. "If we have a patient close to death in the intensive care unit and a liver becomes available, that person will get it, rather than the next one on the list."

That evening, Frank and I discussed our situation. In order to devote so much of my energy to the transplant process and avoid what I then unfortunately viewed as time-wasting grief, I maintained extensive denial about the seriousness of Frank's condition. Because of his astonishing powers of endurance, which enabled him to work full-time when most people would be in a hospital, I was convinced that by sheer force of will Frank would not die until a liver became available for him. "You've been told before you had six months to live," I said to him. "They were wrong then, and I believe they are wrong now."

"Maybe they're not. I'm so jaundiced, and it's getting worse all the time. It can't go on forever like this," Frank replied.

"Even so, you heard what the surgeon said about the sickest people getting moved to the top of the list. If things get really bad, and Dr. Prokupek says there's nothing else he can do, we'll fly here immediately. They'll have to admit you to the ICU and give you the next liver."

In the throes of my denial I couldn't even begin to imagine that only four months later we would be required to put this plan into action.

* * *

We returned home, and while at first things seemed to go on as usual, ominous signs soon became apparent. Over the next few months, Frank needed to be hospitalized twice: first for pneumonia, which destabilized his precarious liver function; and then again for liver failure. By the end of January, although he continued to teach in the classrooms at Challenger, Frank's health was rapidly deteriorating. His abdomen became so swollen with retained fluid that he was forced to go to the emergency room twice to have it drained; his ankles and feet were swollen as well, to the point that he had to leave his shoelaces untied; and his skin was so yellow people stared at him in the street. Dr. Prokupek advised us to get to Pittsburgh while Frank was still able to travel.

We left not one day too soon. While on the flight to Pittsburgh, Frank became confused and nearly comatose; we had to walk up and down the aisles in order for him to remain awake. The recent abdominal drainage sites continued to leak fluid, which soaked his clothes despite the colostomy bags we applied over the area. At least once every hour, Frank and I had to squeeze into the tiny airplane bathroom so I could change them before they overflowed.

An ambulance met us at the Pittsburgh airport and took us to the Medical Center, where Frank was admitted to the Liver Transplant ICU. Within two days, he was comatose and on life support. He never did receive the transplant. On February 13, 1999, Frank died due to hemorrhage into his lungs: a complication of liver failure, and a long-delayed consequence of the trauma and abuse of his childhood. I was devastated by his loss.

* * *

The process of working through my grief over Frank's death was long and difficult, and continues to this day. The overwhelming helplessness and fear I endured throughout the two weeks we spent in the cold and impersonal Liver Transplant ICU added a dimension of horror and trauma that should never be part of the end of life. My experience in Pittsburgh stood in stark contrast to the peace and safety that were the hallmarks of Sonny's final days.

There was also something about the presence of real hope, about the possibility Frank might suddenly and miraculously be cured by receiving a new liver, which complicated my bereavement. It was this, in addition to the practical, often mundane activities required in maximizing Frank's chances for a successful transplant, which distracted me from the important work of anticipatory grief. Because I had accepted the terminal nature of Sonny's condition, I had begun grieving his loss long before the time of his passing. With Frank, I obstinately clung to hope until the moment of his physical death, unable to bear the thought that a treatment existed for his illness which had saved so many others but would not save him.

For Frank, however, the process of seeking a liver transplant was a central vehicle of recovery from his abusive childhood. Through it he came to see (contrary to what he had learned from his family) he was a person of value and deserving of love, and that he could count on those close to him to be there for him. The days before our final trip to Pittsburgh were for him a time of reflection and summing up. "I see so clearly now how the mission applies to me," Frank told me. "I spent my whole life running after my family for a crumb of affection they were totally incapable of giving. If I get a second chance with a new liver, I will do things so differently."

At the end of his life, Frank also had a deep understanding of the commonality of human pain, and the importance of looking under the surface for the true meaning of things. "It's like you and me," he said. "We look so different superficially; you, the educated doctor, and me, the drug dealer with a conscience. But underneath, we are just the same."

Colonnade

History, despite its wrenching pain, cannot be unlived; however,
if faced with courage, it need not be lived again.

—Maya Angelou

CHAPTER FOUR

Trauma Theory: Embracing Our Humanity

*I am afraid to forget. I fear that we human creatures do not forget
cleanly, as the animals presumably do. What protrudes and
does not fit in our pasts rises to haunt us and make us
spiritually unwell in the present.*

—J. Glenn Gray, *The Warriors: Reflections on Men in Battle*

During the years of my desperate quest for relief from pain, I sought out a prominent psychopharmacologist in New York to treat me with medications. It was 1980: I was doing my internal medicine residency in Buffalo. Each week I would fly down to Manhattan to meet with the doctor, who had an impressive office on the Upper East Side, and the Ivy League credentials I so respected at the time. For nearly a year, I took Lithium in addition to an antidepressant; as much as I prayed for this to be what, at last, controlled my "illness," I finally had to admit it was not. Despite much "state of the art" fine-tuning of the medications, my often disabling symptoms continued much as they did before, leading me to the inescapable conclusion I was incurable.

It was around this time that Post-Traumatic Stress Disorder (PTSD), courtesy of the tireless activism of Vietnam veterans, was accepted by the American Psychiatric Association as a recognized condition. In my doctor's defense, there was then no awareness that people could be troubled by the destructive long-term effects of non-combat-related forms of trauma; as well, I did not then view my childhood experiences as "traumatic" and so would not have related them as such. In retrospect, I am not surprised the traditional approach to treatment was unsuccessful.

What I have learned since, through my own recovery work and that of others, is the effects of trauma are *normal human reactions to overwhelming stress, and not a disease or sign of weakness.* In a sense, a fuller understanding of how trauma impacts us physically, psychologically, and spiritually can enable us to appreciate and embrace further dimensions of our humanity. However, we live in a society which, for the most part, celebrates the superficial and views with contempt serious self-examination. The circumstances of human trauma and its consequences, displayed in seemingly bizarre and enigmatic forms of re-enactment, are seen as threatening and repugnant: areas of the human heart and soul better left undisturbed. But if we are concerned with the health and even the longevity of our society, it will be necessary for each of us to put our discomfort aside and examine these areas closely.

* * *

While we may associate the word "trauma" with images of concentration camps, battlefields, and the Twin Towers on 9/11, in reality traumatic experiences (especially those which occur to children in unhealthy family environments) can be extremely subtle, but with similarly devastating long-term effects. Any event or ongoing condition may be considered traumatic *if it overwhelms an individual's ability to cope, rendering them helpless.* For humans, helplessness is one of the worst experiences we can be forced to endure; we are programmed for survival, and situations in which we can do nothing to fight for that survival are extremely difficult for us. In the case of children, who may not have the perspective to realize they are overwhelmed, the consequences may be problems which appear to be without cause, often not clearly surfacing until years later during adulthood.

As much as we may wish to leave these sorts of experiences behind us, human beings have great difficulty in doing so. Even when we are successful in putting the memories of such events firmly out of our awareness, the effects of trauma linger deep beneath the surface, and are expressed in the symbolic language of behavior through the unconscious process of traumatic re-enactment.

My beloved grandson Christian has taught me much about reading the symbolic language of traumatic re-enactment, and about the importance of being present for others in a nonjudgmental way so they can work through their pain to a healthy resolution. Twelve years old at the time I write this, Christian is a brilliant and deeply insightful young man; however, from the time he started school, he learned there was "something wrong" with his handwriting and drawing. At first he knew this because, after comparing his work with his classmates', he noticed that his first and second grade teachers would display his artwork and essays in the least conspicuous places in the room, if at all. As time went on, his teachers' displeasure with his work became more overt, and from comments made in his presence and in front of his peers (such as that he was lazy and would have better handwriting if only he applied himself more, or that because he persisted in coloring outside the lines, perhaps he wasn't able to learn as well as the other children), he felt shame, hurt, and anger. To make matters worse, he felt unsafe at school, as his teachers would frequently yell at him and the other children in a shaming manner for minor infractions of classroom rules.

During his second grade year, I would pick Christian up from school several days each week and be present with him as he did his homework. I soon noticed, although we had a very close and trusting relationship, it was becoming increasingly difficult for me to ensure he completed his assignments, especially if they included writing or drawing. Even with my understanding of human trauma, it was several months before I realized what was going on, and how it needed to be dealt with. Then, the day came when Christian categorically refused to write, dropping his pencil as he sat across from me with his head down, staring at the floor.

"Christian," I said calmly, "when you refuse to write, what is it you are trying to say?"

He looked up at me and answered directly and without hesitation: "I'm saying I hate that school, and I wish I could blow it up!"

It is a testament to the strength of Christian's trust in me that he was able to be so honest, and underscores the absolute necessity for all of us to have safe people in our lives, so this process of working through pain can take place. (Even as a small child, Christian knew students had carried out acts of great violence at schools, and making this statement to the wrong person could have dire consequences for him.) Of equal importance is that each of us develops our ability to read the symbolic language underlying the behavior of others, so we can recognize unconscious traumatic re-enactment and respond effectively, with clarity and compassion.

At this point, I felt much relief that we were now going to be able to get to the bottom of the issue. Christian had taken the first critical step: putting words to that which he had previously expressed only through behavior. "I am so sorry you have been feeling such pain," I said. "Would you tell me more about that?"

In the weeks to come Christian and I talked often about how he felt being shamed and disrespected by his teacher; he also expressed his hurt and rage through safe forms of externalization, such as tearing up old phone books. By working through this experience, Christian came to see the worst part of it was he had been helpless. That, however, was about to change.

One day when I arrived at his classroom, Christian was completing a coloring assignment he had been given. He had used the same yellow crayon to color each of the pictures, and had obviously made no effort to keep inside the lines.

"See my work?" he said. "I'm going to take this up to the teacher right now, and tell her this is my assignment, and I colored outside the lines not because there is anything wrong with me, but because it is how I express who I am."

I squeezed myself into Christian's tiny desk to watch this momentous interaction. He was polite and respectful to his teacher as he handed in his assignment and repeated his statement. When he was done, he turned to me with an expression of immense joy and satisfaction; I stood up, and he ran to me, jumped into my arms, and we danced around the room while his teacher watched speechlessly.

That day, Christian took back his power. And as he has often told me since, that experience changed his life. Now fully conscious of the meaning of the symbolic language of his behavior ("I feel hurt and angry when you shame and disrespect me") he knows he re-enacted his trauma not because he was bad, lazy, or weak; he did so because he is human. He also now knows there is a way to work through trauma: and while it may not be easy or pleasant, it is ultimately exhilarating and liberating.

One of my own experiences with traumatic re-enactment still astonishes me with the extraordinarily unconscious nature and power of this process, and how difficult it can be to interpret our own symbolic language. In late 1996, I awoke early one morning from a sound sleep in the most agonizing pain of my life. It was most severe on the right side of my back, and radiated around on the same side to my abdomen and down to my groin. When, after a short time I could feel no improvement, I became desperate and terrified, and called a friend to drive me to the emergency room.

In the emergency room, a nurse gave me an injection of morphine through a needle she had placed in my arm. Rather than pain relief, the drug caused me to have a feeling of suffocation in my chest, which frightened me greatly. I told the nurse about it, but she seemed unconcerned, and disregarded my request to make a note on my chart I was not to have any more injections of narcotics through the IV.

After X-rays and urine tests diagnosed my problem as a kidney stone, I was admitted to the hospital. That night, the pain returned. I asked the nurse on duty for oral pain medication, but she told me all that was ordered was morphine through the IV. I explained I didn't want any IV narcotics, and requested she call the doctor to approve an oral medication. She refused, however, insisting that morphine doesn't cause the kind of side effect I described, and she wasn't going to disturb the doctor in the middle of the night when there was pain medication already ordered for me.

I lay there in agony in my hospital bed and felt overwhelmingly helpless. I thought about calling a taxi to take me home, but then I would just be alone in my house with that unbearable pain. Finally, it was morning. A new nurse came in and told me I was scheduled that day for a cystoscopy (an invasive procedure in which the urinary tract is examined and kidney stones removed through a scope). "I didn't give my permission for that," I informed her. "You'll have to discuss it with your doctor," she replied. "Meanwhile, we're holding your breakfast."

Later that morning the urologist came to see me; I told him I wanted to go home and see if the stone would pass on its own. He gave me a prescription for oral pain medication, and I left the hospital as quickly as I could. The next day, I must have passed the stone, because the really severe pain was gone.

But the helplessness of that night continued to be expressed through persistent pain and discomfort in the area where the kidney stone had been. Over the next eighteen months, I sought help from many doctors, had three cystoscopies, a stent placed in (and removed from) my ureter, and numerous X-rays and scans; but even after all of this, the cause of my chronic pain remained elusive. Finally, at the Mayo Clinic I had a laparoscopy, another invasive procedure in which the abdomen is examined through a scope. This was completely normal, as all my other tests had been. The surgeon, however, a wise and caring man, cured my pain on the spot with a simple question. "Did it ever occur to you," he asked, "that trauma can become imprinted on the brain and then expressed by physical symptoms?"

The truth of this statement resonated within me the moment I heard it. From that point forward, I had no more pain. I had finally been able to make conscious the symbolic language of my body.

In a primal way, my body had been remembering how I had lain in a hospital bed in extreme agony, receiving no form of relief either from the medication (which really only further traumatized me) or from the human staff whose uncaring attitude cemented home the fundamental message of the experience: I was helpless. Until the moment came when words were able to describe the trauma, allowing me to begin to reclaim my power over the ordeal, I remained helpless.

Since then, I have had several more kidney stones, but never again chronic phantom kidney stone pain. Now, when I get a kidney stone, I know exactly what to do: stay home, take oral pain medication which I always keep on hand, and drink water. It was the helplessness, not the intensity of the pain, which brought about the traumatic re-enactment.

Sometimes, as in my kidney stone episode, traumatic re-enactment is connected to a specific overwhelming event. Frequently, however, it manifests as a lifelong pattern of behavior in response to a childhood during which we absorb, in a deep and experiential way, the immutable fact of our own helplessness. In such situations, we may be unconsciously drawn to activities involving risk-taking and self-injury in order to express through symbolic language the struggle to regain our own power.

During my internship year, I learned to ride a motorcycle. In a time in which the sleep deprivation and stressful work of my medical training compounded my pre-existing issues, motorcycle riding provided brief respites from my anguish. In the days before mandatory helmets, and before I officially obtained my license, I would speed on the freeways of upstate New York, relishing the oblivion of risk taking. Even the threat of being banned from ever receiving a license (as occurred when I was pulled over for speeding and it was discovered that I was riding illegally) did not dampen my enthusiasm. While I hired an attorney to plead my case, I continued to ride unlicensed until I went to court. The lure of even temporary relief from intolerable emotional pain can be exceedingly strong, as it was for me, overriding both judgment and conscience.

Two years later, in the middle of an especially harsh winter, I rode my motorcycle from upstate New York to Texas to visit some friends from medical school. All went well until I stopped for gas in a small town about 150 miles from Houston, my final destination. It was raining hard, and I had just turned out of the gas station when I slid on some wet gravel. I landed on my right side, with the brunt of the impact on my shoulder, which, after the initial shock wore off, began to hurt very badly. As my shoulder wouldn't move on its own, I had to use my left arm to place my right hand back onto the handlebars. In excruciating pain, I rode the remaining distance to Houston. As soon as I arrived, I went to the emergency room, as by this time my entire right arm was extremely swollen and bruised. When an X-ray showed my arm had been broken, I felt elated in a strange way I did not then understand.

For years, I would tell this story with pride as a sort of badge of courage, without any awareness of what my symbolic language actually revealed about me. The reality was, both risk-taking and enduring unconsciously self-inflicted pain alleviated my constant gnawing sense of helplessness by providing the illusion that I was brave, strong, and could tolerate anything. As I progressed in my trauma recovery work, I came to see the many areas of my life in which I used risk-taking and self-injury (sometimes quite subtly) to express the horror of the helplessness of my past, and to protect myself from seeing the truth. When I first committed to giving up these behaviors, I realized how insidious and almost addictive they were, often creeping back in even as I consciously tried my hardest to keep them out. Still today, I must exercise vigilance to prevent myself from falling back into these old trauma-driven patterns.

If we only look at the surface, risk-taking and self-injurious behaviors may seem bizarre and confusing. It can be disturbing to hear about children who hit and choke themselves, teenagers who cut themselves with knives, and adults who engage in masochistic sexual practices. It can be disconcerting to think about the dark side of risk-taking inherent in criminal activities.

We can, however, gain much wisdom about the nature of humanity if we put aside our initial fears and judgments about such behaviors and instead ask ourselves what it is that is being communicated. The truth is, through even the most grotesque and appalling forms of behavioral traumatic re-enactment, we express the fundamental nature of what it means to be human. Our need for unconditional love, for safe and nurturing connections with others, and for freedom and autonomy are all themes in the human medium of symbolic language.

The concepts of trauma theory (a body of science-based information which explains the universal human response to trauma) can help us to understand more about the driving forces underlying such self-destructive and anti-social behaviors, and why they take the particular forms that they do. With such awareness, we are better equipped to be present in a compassionate and healing manner, for ourselves as well as for others, no matter how mystifying such behavior may seem.

* * *

Traumatic re-enactment is a uniquely human process, and it has much to do with the intricacy and complexity of the human brain: specifically, with our capacity for language, and with the split between our two distinct memory systems. Because our more sophisticated and recently evolved verbally-based memory system functions poorly in situations of severe stress, trauma-related memories are often stored in our more primitive, nonverbal memory system. Memories in this primal system, which are unattached to words and usually take the form of images, strong emotions, and physical sensations, can only be expressed through behavior. Even when we have clear recall of an overpowering experience and can describe it in words, elements of it remain in our primitive memory; therefore, we will continue to express it through behavior until we have worked it through and become conscious of its deeper meanings. In a sense, the human response to trauma is so complicated because of the co-existence of our primitive brain (where trauma is processed) with our higher mental functions, which allow for responses which are sophisticated and creative as well as highly cryptic.

Christian's and my stories are only a few examples of the vast range of human behaviors, both self-destructive and anti-social, in which we unconsciously engage as a consequence of unprocessed traumatic experience. These commonly include drug addiction, alcoholism, violence, gang life, risk-taking (including crime), self-injury, eating disorders, compulsive activities (including sex, work, gambling, and others), unhealthy relationships, and insensitivity and lack of empathy (which includes racism and hate). While it may intuitively make sense that positive or healthy activities are absent from this list, there is a reason we are drawn to specific behaviors, and once again it has to do with our unique human neurobiology.

For most of human history, we existed as hunter-gatherers in a dangerous and violent environment against which we had few defenses. Similar to other mammals, to aid in our survival we are equipped with a basic internal protective mechanism, the "fight or flight" response, as it was called when first described in 1929 by the American physiologist Walter Cannon. When we are faced with danger, the thalamus (an area in our primal brain) stimulates the adrenal gland to produce hormones such as epinephrine, which bring about physiological changes facilitating spontaneous actions related to combat or escape. In such traumatic situations, we are in an agitated and hyperaroused state; we also experience physical sensations we associate with extreme anxiety, such as palpitations, rapid breathing, and fear.

Through the more recent research of British psychologist Jeffrey Gray, important advances have occurred in our understanding of this basic human protective mechanism. We now know there are four distinct stages in this innate response to danger (rather than two), which take place in the following sequence: "Freeze, flight, fight, and fright."

The initial impulse to "freeze" (remain completely still) has survival advantage because being "frozen" helps us to avoid detection by predators, who may see motion more easily than color. Also, during this stage we are exceptionally alert and vigilant, readying us to deal most effectively with the threat. The next two phases actually occur in the order opposite that originally thought by Walter Cannon: we are first instinctively impelled to "flee," and only turn and "fight" after all other available options have been exhausted. The final stage in this sequence is "fright," or tonic immobility ("playing dead"), which occurs when the situation escalates to the point at which we have physical contact with the predator. The survival advantage of this response is that tonic immobility may lead the predator (who may assume we are dead) to temporarily loosen its grip, providing an opportunity for escape.

There is a definite disconnect between the hard-wired nature of our human response to danger and societal expectations of how we are "supposed" to behave in threatening situations. It may be helpful to understand that fighting before fleeing, as soldiers are trained to do during war, is in opposition to our evolved instinctual response, and this inner conflict serves to increase the stress, intensity, and subsequent traumatic aftereffects of combat. Awareness that the "fright" response is physiologically programmed into us as an integral part of being human (and can enhance our ability to survive) may enable us to exercise compassion, rather than berate ourselves as cowards, when we react passively in the face of violence or sexual assault.

The pituitary gland and hypothalamus (also areas of our primitive brain) produce endorphins: related to heroin and morphine, these substances, too, are important in our response to danger. By relieving pain from injury, they can assist in a successful escape; they also counteract the effects of epinephrine and help to alleviate the unpleasant manifestations of hyperarousal once the threat has passed.

While this system is highly effective when danger is sporadic, it causes serious problems when we are in situations of continuous or repetitive trauma, such as combat, imprisonment, domestic violence, and child abuse. Because the threat is ongoing, we are in a state of chronic hyperarousal, which we as humans experience as an enormously distressing and destructive condition. It should not be at all surprising, then, that those of us so afflicted would be drawn to activities which calm this unbearable sense of agitation by stimulating endorphin production, such as drug and alcohol addiction, violence and gang life, risk-taking and crime, binging and purging, self-harm, and compulsive behaviors (e.g., work, sex, and exercise).

It may at first seem antithetical that these behaviors, especially violence, risk-taking, crime, and self-harm, could have any sort of calming effect. Many experts believe we can actually become addicted to stressful experiences because of the disturbed functioning of our internal endorphin (or opioid) system caused by exposure to habitual trauma. In such circumstances, we become accustomed to abnormally high circulating levels of endorphins, which are produced in response to the chronic hyperarousal of ongoing stress. When the external threat is relieved, endorphin levels decline, leaving us once again feeling agitated; to alleviate this anguish, we unconsciously seek out stressful situations (such as risk-taking) which will, after an initial burst of hyperarousal, result in increased production of endorphins.

The underlying commonality among these activities, which are seemingly diametrically opposed (as in violence and self-harm) and unrelated (as in crime and eating disorders), is that they all cause alterations in our endorphin system which temporarily ease the misery of chronic trauma. Which of these modalities of pain avoidance we incorporate appears to depend on many factors, including what is modeled to us in our environment by other traumatized individuals, our genetic predisposition to issues such as chemical dependency, and what we find to be most effective in mitigating our suffering. Chronic hyperarousal also interferes with our ability to make sound decisions, solve problems, and control our impulses, compounding the destruction to self and others caused by these trauma-driven behaviors.

These concepts can help us understand why siblings, growing up in the same family environment and subject to the same traumatic situations, may follow what superficially appear to be very different life paths. Rather than an indication of the relative merits or goodness of the siblings, this is instead a reflection of their individual tendencies toward more or less socially acceptable methods of chronic hyperarousal management.

This is illustrated by the life-long difficulties faced by two acquaintances of mine. George and his sister Louise grew up in a family whose superficial health belied many destructive secrets. Their parents took great pains to make the family appear as perfect as possible: they attended church every week, volunteered at the homeless shelter, and decorated their house each Christmas with the most elaborate light display in town. No one suspected that beneath this veneer of normalcy existed an appalling degree of domestic violence, spurred by their father's alcoholism. Throughout their childhood, George and Louise lived in a miserable state of chronic hyperarousal, unable to let their guard down for an instant because they never knew when the next violent onslaught would begin.

From the start, George had problems in school. He had difficulty sitting still and focusing on his work, and was frequently disruptive in class. Because the school officials accepted without further investigation his parents' version of a stable home life, they concluded that there must be "something wrong" with George. He was diagnosed with Attention Deficit Hyperactivity Disorder (ADHD), put on medication, and shunted to special education classes. No one saw the truth of the situation: that because of his trauma-driven chronic hyperarousal, George could not tolerate a calm classroom environment, needing instead to unconsciously generate stress to increase his levels of circulating endorphins, thereby alleviating his anguish.

The course of George's life is reflective of the fact that he never received help in working through his trauma, and that he continued to live in daily terror of violence at home. Having absorbed the message that he wasn't smart and would never succeed in school, he dropped out in the eleventh grade, not long after discovering that drugs were, for him, an even more powerful inducer of endorphin production than acting out in the classroom. After leaving school, George's drug use escalated. Before long he was burglarizing stores, an activity which in itself became an addiction of sorts, the risk-taking of crime providing additional temporary relief from the affliction of chronic hyperarousal. Recently released from prison, George is attempting to work through the impact of his childhood trauma on his life, as he struggles with his addiction to drugs and crime.

Louise, who was subjected to the same terrifying experiences during her childhood, was drawn to different forms of hyperarousal-calming activities. For this reason, on the surface, her life appears less obviously trauma-driven than her brother's. In part because of the developmental advantage of little girls in adapting to the classroom environment, Louise had positive early academic experiences, and soon came to view school as a place of refuge from the violence in her home. She always received excellent grades, as she was unconsciously drawn to spending long hours studying in the library, alleviating as it did the distressing hyperarousal which consumed her at home. In high school she expanded the roster of activities which served this purpose: she was on the basketball and track teams, had a role in every school play, worked on the school newspaper, and belonged to the chess and history clubs. When she was accepted by a prestigious university and moved out of her parents' house, Louise fully believed that she was leaving the horror of her childhood behind her forever. She considered George a loser because he lacked the strength of character to deal with his problems in a constructive and positive way, as she had done.

As expected, Louise graduated from college and then law school with the highest honors, continuing her compulsive pattern of excessive work throughout these years. After graduation, she was offered a position in a powerful New York corporate law firm, where she once again was very successful, working with her clients late into the evenings seven days a week. Within two years, Louise became one of the youngest partners in the history of the firm. She rarely thought of her difficult childhood, or of her brother George, with whom she had only minimal contact; she was convinced that through diligence and hard work she had eliminated any lingering effects of the trauma of her past.

Everything changed for Louise when, ten years later, she fractured both her legs in a serious car accident and was disabled for six months. For the first time in her adult life, she was unable to work compulsively to calm her hyperarousal, and she became unbearably agitated and anxious. Louise found the pain pills her doctor had prescribed provided temporary relief from her emotional anguish; she began taking more and more of them, and was soon addicted. After she returned to work, Louise was too impacted by drug addiction to function effectively, and it was not long before she was given a choice by her partners: resign or enter a substance abuse treatment program. It was an agonizing decision for Louise, who was forced to confront the painful truth that her response to trauma was not very different from that of her brother George. She chose to begin treatment; through the process of recovery from drug addiction, she began for the first time to examine the huge impact her traumatic childhood had on her life.

* * *

Two weeks after Frank's death, I returned to the Catalyst office for the first time. It was a Saturday morning, a time I had specifically chosen because, in my intense grief, I was not yet ready to see my co-workers. However, I had forgotten that occasionally we did HIV prevention programs at Challenger on Saturdays, a fact of which I was abruptly reminded when Jackie, one of our health educators, drove into the parking lot just as I was getting out of my car.

A young woman with AIDS, Jackie had worked with Frank and me for the past few years on our HIV prevention program for incarcerated teens; along with other members of our team, she was continuing this work while Frank and I were away in Pittsburgh. The three of us shared a kind of multileveled friendship: sometimes surface (Frank built a new gate in Jackie's back yard) and sometimes deeper (Jackie was one of the first people in whom we confided that we loved one another). As Frank's health deteriorated, and we arranged for our emergency trip to Pittsburgh, I could tell Jackie needed to keep her interactions with us on the most superficial level possible; this was made even clearer when she wrote, "Stay cool, man! Party in Steel Town!" on a card from all of our co-workers, sent to Frank while he was on life support in the Liver Transplant ICU. And, synchronicity being what it is, Jackie was the first person to whom I was going to have to speak at the Catalyst office.

She grabbed the box of educational materials out of her car and followed me into the office. "We had such a great class today, Susan!" she said to me, as if she had seen me only yesterday and nothing tragic had just happened.

For a moment I wondered if it was possible Jackie hadn't heard Frank had died. So I asked her if she knew.

"Oh yes, I heard," she responded in a strange, neutral tone. I think she was hoping I wouldn't bring it up: that I would pretend, as she was doing, that it did not happen, that Frank did not die. That I would just go back to working with the incarcerated teens as if there had never been a person named Frank Altadonna.

Jackie busied herself by putting away her materials, clearly done with her conversation with me. I went into my office, shut the door, put my head down on my desk, and sobbed. It had not been an auspicious beginning.

* * *

Each of has an immense ability to influence others, although we are for the most part unaware of it. Even in the briefest of human contacts, we have the power to bring healing to a hurting person simply by being present with them: but we cannot do this if we are still driven by our own traumatic pasts. This heartbreaking interaction illustrates the devastation that unhealed trauma can create; in this case, through the unconscious process of dissociation.

Dissociation is a uniquely human mechanism by which we protect ourselves from unbearable emotional pain. Most humans operate at peak efficiency as an integrated whole, with the mental functions of memory, consciousness, identity, and awareness of the environment all working cooperatively. When we dissociate, we unconsciously separate these processes, which prevents us from knowing what is too overwhelming to know, or from feeling what is too overwhelming to feel. There are many forms of dissociation, ranging from fainting (complete cessation of consciousness), total amnesia for our identity (fugue state), and amnesia for specific events or for large portions of our childhood, to the everyday human activities of daydreaming and "going on auto-pilot" when driving. Dissociation is not always pathological, and probably evolved because it was a survival advantage for humans to be able to multitask, as well as to engage in creative thinking.

One of the most universal ways in which humans dissociate is to separate an experience from our consciousness of our feelings about that experience; in its most extreme form, this is referred to as "emotional numbing." As with acute flight or fight response and chronic hyperarousal, in situations of immediate trauma, dissociation from our feelings can be lifesaving; however, in the long term, it becomes a serious liability to our own health as well as to society as a whole. Unconscious avoidance of painful truths can result in the severe narrowing of the scope and quality of our lives. This proved sadly true with Jackie when, in the months following Frank's death, she withdrew from all of the programs, activities, and friendships at Catalyst in which she had previously been involved and which had held great meaning for her. Also, as in Jackie's case, when we are unable, due to our own unprocessed trauma, to be present for others who are in pain, it contributes to the perpetuation of the insensitivity, lack of empathy, and lost opportunities for healing that are so prevalent in our society.

* * *

We take for granted the impact of trauma on individuals. Most of us know someone who, following an abusive childhood, becomes addicted to drugs, or is involved in one battering relationship after another; we accept this as "the way of things." What is less clear is that trauma-driven behaviors, when carried out on an enormous scale by millions of hurting people, create the paradigm by which our society functions. The cumulative result of these pain-driven behaviors can be seen in the many scourges of modern life: in our violent and crime-ridden society; in the ongoing cycle of child abuse and neglect; in unemployment, homelessness, and poverty; in the epidemics of

AIDS, Hepatitis C, drug addiction and alcoholism; and, on an international level, in terrorism and war.

Trauma-driven behaviors and activities, no matter how purposeful, heartwrenching, repugnant, or evil they may appear on the surface, are all ways in which human beings struggle to cope with unbearable pain. The same process is operating within a homeless addict and a workaholic executive; in an inner city gang member and an anorexic young woman; and in a violent criminal and a self-injuring teenager. Some forms of traumatic re-enactment are more socially acceptable than others, which for some of us is license to condemn those individuals who engage in forms of re-enactment that frighten or endanger us, while offering sympathy and support for those we feel are more "deserving." All trauma-driven behavior serves the same purpose; and in our universal response to trauma we are all connected, regardless of our superficial differences such as race, religion, or gender. Once we understand this, we will be more able to feel compassion for those among us, including ourselves, who live with the heartbreaking consequences of trauma; and we may also be inspired to create a society which accepts the process of healing from trauma as a normal part of human life.

All Things Must Pass

*It is only with the heart that one can see rightly;
what is essential is invisible to the eye.*

—Antoine de Saint-Exupery

CHAPTER FIVE

Unhealthy Attachment: The Hidden Wound

*The desolation and terror of, for the first time, realizing that the
mother can lose you, or you her, and your own abysmal
loneliness and helplessness without her.*
—Francis Thompson

Frank possessed a generosity of spirit which simply radiated compassion, caring, and unconditional love. This was all the more remarkable considering his early experiences of neglect and abandonment, and was one of the many reasons I admired, respected, and loved him so much.

This extraordinary quality was perhaps best reflected in Frank's attitude towards Sonny. Throughout the years we worked together as colleagues and close friends (before we knew we loved each other), Frank heard me share Sonny's story hundreds of times. He would later reveal he often felt intimidated by this, and despaired of ever having a deeper relationship with me. "I felt I could never compete with a love story that powerful," he told me.

With time, Frank came to understand competition was unnecessary, and realized he, too, felt connected to Sonny. To my boundless delight, Frank loved Sonny and included him in our relationship. He became a surrogate grandfather to Christian, and the three of us made frequent trips to Southern California zoos, aquariums, and amusement parks. He often accompanied me to the cemetery; in an indelible memory, I can still see him, on a stormy, bitterly cold Christmas Eve (which was, unbeknownst to us, our last visit there together), kneeling on Sonny's grave, resolutely nailing a wreath into the frozen ground. And he developed his personal form of spiritual communication with Sonny, which intensified as the time of his own death approached.

"If we're all going to be married together, we should all be buried together," Frank used to say, and indeed we planned (in my denial, of course, sometime far in the future) that Frank and I would both be cremated and buried in Sonny's and my cemetery plot. I loved this idea, as it was symbolic of my deep attachment to both of them.

Several days before our emergency trip to Pittsburgh, when his liver was rapidly failing, Frank talked to me about his wishes in case he did not survive the transplant. It was early in the morning, and we lay in bed, held hands, and had one of the most intimate conversations of our lives. I put aside the terror of his loss which drove my denial and was able to be fully present with him; that is, until the subject of his burial desires came up.

"I guess I should be buried in my family's plot, next to my mother," Frank told me.

In that instant, I felt horrendously abandoned, an emotion so overpowering it precluded rational thought. "I thought we were all going to be buried together in Sonny's cemetery plot!" I nearly screamed.

"I know, but I don't think my family would understand that. I should probably do what would be easiest for them." Frank's voice sounded flat and hopeless, as it always did when he was yearning for the loving family he would never have.

"I can't believe I'm hearing this!" I cried. "They've abandoned you your entire life, and yet you always run back to them. I just don't understand!"

As was usual for me when I felt abandoned, I was overcome by a violent and uncontrollable impulse to get away from the situation. Without any consciousness of what was driving the intensity of my response (or even that I had ceased to be present for Frank and was, in fact, abandoning him in his time of greatest vulnerability and need), I angrily turned away, got out of bed, and began to stalk out of the room. I stopped abruptly, however, when I heard Frank's voice.

"Susan," he said softly. "Don't run away."

Something about being called so clearly and compassionately on the truth of my behavior immediately defused my anguish. I apologized to Frank, got back into bed, and we resumed our conversation. He went on to tell me that what he really wanted was to be cremated and have his ashes scattered from the Brooklyn Bridge.

"Why didn't you ever tell me this before?" I asked him.

"A part of me still didn't believe that anyone would really do this for me," Frank said, "because that's what I learned from my family. I guess I am still learning that not everybody is like my family. Also, I knew how much it meant to you that the three of us be buried together, and I didn't want to hurt you. But I trust you, and I know if you make a promise to me, you will keep it."

Frank's wishes were honored at a memorial service held at sunrise on the Brooklyn Bridge on September 19, 1999. Not surprisingly, Frank's family continued to treat him in death as they had treated him in life. The service was attended exclusively by his friends from California, who flew to New York especially for the occasion. Frank's sisters, who lived in New York within an hour's drive from the Brooklyn Bridge, were absent.

Though the surface manifestations differed, Frank and I were both deeply affected by unhealthy attachment with our families. Frank longed for a close bond with his family, and never completely gave up hope that someday this dream might be realized; although at the end of his life he achieved a more realistic view of these circumstances and was able to grieve for that which he never had. In contrast, I dedicated my early life to escaping from a family situation which terrified and overwhelmed me, destroying any possibility of closeness. The truth is, even today, I feel little emotion about my family, and have no desire to reunite with them. The effects of unhealthy attachment persist in this area of my life, making it difficult for me to understand (other than intellectually) how people, like Frank and Sonny, can remain connected to their families even in the face of horrifying abuse or neglect. Dealing with abandonment issues in close relationships is another area of ongoing challenge for me which has its roots in unhealthy attachment. Such situations seem to re-create the all-consuming pain I must have felt as a child (but am unconscious of now) when I was emotionally abandoned by my family.

Trauma recovery is a process rather than a state of completion. Writing this book brought to my attention, in a very direct way, the continuing impact of unhealthy attachment on important aspects of my life. I am committed to working through this issue, no matter how painful it may be, because I know it will ultimately result in more personal peace and clarity, as well more ability to contribute to the healing of others. While I am not sure what the practical outcome will be regarding contact or reconciliation with my family, it is my hope that doing this work will enable me to gain compassion for them through an understanding of the pain which drove their behavior, just as I have come to have compassion for myself and others. Perhaps all of this remained hidden from my awareness for so long because of the subtle nature of the devastation caused by unhealthy attachment.

* * *

Like our other basic internal protective mechanisms, human attachment behavior evolved because it was important to our survival. In the hostile world in which we existed as primitive humans, one of our primary defenses against outside threats was to ensure safety in numbers through a cohesive social group. One purpose of attachment behavior was the maintenance of such a group. Although our environment has changed immensely, our need for others is still evident today in the highly social nature of our species, and in the detrimental effects on humans of prolonged isolation.

We have the longest period of helplessness and dependency of any mammal on earth; for this reason, attachment bonds with our parents (or caregivers) are especially important in ensuring our survival. The reciprocal and enduring emotional and physical connection that defines attachment keeps us close to our caregivers for protection, while at the same time allowing us to explore and learn within a safe context in order to grow into healthy adults. Despite our society's glorification of independence and self-reliance, the truth is we are absolutely unable to develop normally without loving and protective attachments; the formidable task of healing as an adult from the effects of unhealthy attachments illustrates the intensely primal nature of this instinct. Attachment behavior is universal; it serves the same purpose for all human beings, regardless of culture, race, religion, or gender. As with the human response to trauma, an awareness of human attachment needs can transcend our superficial differences and be a source of mutual understanding, compassion, and connection for us all.

Because the purpose of human attachment is survival, it makes intuitive sense that we bond more closely to those around us when we are frightened or under attack. This is true even when the source of the danger is from within our social group instead of from outside forces: that is, from our caregivers, those who are supposed to protect us. We may feel this attachment much more intensely when the threat from our caregivers is not constant, but interspersed with periods of safety and warmth, as is the case in many abusive homes. This is the cause of trauma-bonding, in which we unconsciously absorb, through our attachment to and interactions with our caregivers, the message that violence and emotional abuse are normal parts of human relationships. That there is such a desperate need for domestic violence shelters in our society is a testament to the inordinate power of the trauma bond and the extent of its impact.

When, as children, we have secure attachments with our caregivers, we learn to soothe ourselves when we experience overwhelming emotions. In the normal course of childhood development, we venture away from the safe base of the adults to explore our environment. When we are frightened (hyperaroused) by these new experiences, we run back to our caregivers to be comforted by them. There is a growing body of evidence that, through countless repetitions of this scenario, our developing brains actually learn to produce the correct balance of endorphins to counteract the "flight or fight" response which occurs when we are distressed. What this ultimately enables us to do is manage our own stress, contain our own intense emotions, and *calm our own hyperarousal.* What this also means is that when our caregivers are unable to be present with us and provide reliable comforting (because of their own trauma-related and attachment issues, substance abuse, mental or physical illness, etc.) we cannot develop this ability. The resulting chronic hyperarousal caused by unhealthy attachment has the same devastating consequences to individuals and society as the more obvious forms of trauma, such as rape and other forms of violence.

What perpetuates this state of affairs within families, generation after generation, is the fact that the sequelae of unhealthy attachment have profound effects on our abilities to be effective parents. Raising emotionally healthy children is challenging under the best of circumstances, but when we have difficulty handling intense feelings, dealing with stressful situations, having patience with and empathy for others, or are actively engaging in anti-social and self-destructive behaviors to calm our own hyperarousal, it is all but impossible. Even when we are aware of our own childhood traumas and are determined not to abuse or neglect our children similarly, without the willingness and commitment to examine our own attachment patterns we will unconsciously re-enact our trauma through our parenting styles in the subtlest of ways. In matters such as these, the subtlest of wounds are often the most perplexing, leaving us wondering what could have gone wrong, defensively blaming our children for their shortcomings and pitying ourselves for what they have become: because everything about their upbringing looked so right, but only on the surface.

A woman I know named Sarah exemplifies this situation. Sarah comes from a background of severe abuse and deprivation. The only child of two wounded individuals (who themselves grew up in circumstances of extreme neglect), from a very young age she was often left alone at home while her parents sought relief from their own hyperarousal through alcohol and drugs. Sarah herself struggled with alcoholism for many years but has been sober for over a decade, a fact of which she is rightly proud. The first in her family to graduate from college, she has a responsible, high paying job, and is now working on her Master's degree. Sarah is a single mother with two children (a circumstance which is, in itself, the result of the unconscious re-enactment of her trauma through compulsive and risky sexual activity). Despite her heavy work responsibilities, she attends all of her children's school events and extracurricular activities, and always puts great effort into making sure that birthdays and holidays are fun-filled celebrations, complete with beautiful decorations and elaborate material gifts.

When her daughter was about three years old, Sarah confided in me, "I just have no patience with Melissa when she has a nightmare and wakes me up with her crying in the middle of the night. I'm tired and stressed, and if I don't get my sleep I won't be any good at work the next day."

"So, how do you comfort her when she has a nightmare?" I asked her.

"I don't comfort her. I tell her to go back to her bed and go to sleep, that it is only a dream and she probably won't even remember it in the morning. You have no idea how hard it is to be a single parent and to have to deal with work and kids and everything else."

When I spent more time with Sarah and her children, I could see that self-absorption and lack of empathy were common patterns in her parenting style. Another time, when she was frantically getting the house ready for guests who were due to arrive any minute, her two-year-old son very hesitantly approached her and informed her he had wet the bed.

"God damn it, Michael!" Sarah shouted at him. "I just did five loads of laundry! Can't you be more careful? Don't you know we have company coming?" Michael's little face twisted with shame and he burst into tears. Sarah continued her whirlwind of preparations, seemingly oblivious to her son's distress; while Melissa, alleviating her own helplessness over these events, aggressively rushed over to caretake her little brother. It was a heartwrenching scene to witness.

A few years later, when Sarah discovered Melissa had been calming her own hyperarousal by drinking alcohol with older boys after school, she immediately took action and arranged for therapy for both her children. However, she quickly changed therapists when it became clear the focus of the work was going to be on her childhood issues and how they impacted her parenting abilities. "That therapist doesn't have any children of her own," Sarah complained to me. "How could she know what it's like? I struggle so hard to be a good mother. I've turned my life around and broken the cycle, and I don't want anyone telling me otherwise! I need a therapist who will deal with my kids' problems. I've done more than enough already to deal with mine. Drugs and alcohol are everywhere these days and then there's all that peer pressure. It's not my fault that she's drinking."

Despite her impressive external achievements and the undeniably positive changes she has been able to create for herself, a critical area of Sarah's life continues to be driven by unresolved trauma; and because of the extraordinarily subtle nature of attachment issues, she is unable to see that it is impacting her children significantly. When we are very small, it is through our attachment to and interactions with our caregivers that we learn about ourselves, our value as people, and how we should relate to others. As this is our only frame of reference, we come to accept whatever we learn in this way as normal, no matter how unpleasant it may feel. We simply may not know there are healthier alternatives to the way things have always been done in our families, and problems with managing intense feelings and stressful situations can challenge our attempts to try out new options. It is particularly difficult if our caregivers were immersed in their own problems and were unable to respond compassionately to our feelings and needs. When this happens, we may have unconsciously absorbed their pattern of self-centeredness and may never have learned to recognize the feelings of others or how to treat them with patience and empathy. It is her self-centeredness, which she views as a normal way of being, that keeps Sarah from the awareness of just how serious a disability it is and how deeply it affects her children. To her it seems unimportant, especially when compared with the striking progress she has made in other areas of her life. Unfortunately, the challenge has now been passed to Melissa and Michael to work through the destructive impact of Sarah's attachment difficulties before they go on to have children of their own.

* * *

For many of us, we were hurt not by what was done to us, but by what we did not receive: unconditional love. There is much misconception about the nature of unconditional love: that it is something of which mere humans are incapable; that it can only come from the divine; or that it is equivalent to putting up with abuse or disrespect from others. These couldn't be further from the truth. We exercise unconditional love when we are able to put aside, for a time, our own feelings and needs in order to be fully present with another person.

We also exercise unconditional love (as well as demonstrate respect) when we allow others, in an age- and circumstance-appropriate manner, to manage the responsibilities of life which rightly belong to them. Caretaking and rescuing a competent individual (as opposed as being a caregiver to someone in a time of need), is not a manifestation of unconditional love; rather, it is a form of traumatic re-enactment in which we unconsciously focus our energy and attention on another, so as to avoid awareness of what is going on emotionally for us.

The rarity of unconditional love, as well as the widespread lack of understanding of its true nature, is connected to the prevalence of unhealed trauma in our world. It is virtually impossible for us to provide our children with unconditional love on a consistent basis when we ourselves are so deeply impacted by our own attachment issues and unprocessed traumas. It is similarly difficult to manifest unconditional love when we have difficulty managing stress, coping with intense emotions, showing empathy for others, or when we are using drugs, alcohol, violence, and other behaviors to calm our hyperarousal.

A more practical (and perhaps somewhat less spiritual) way to think about unconditional love is that it is a manner of relating with our children that meets their basic developmental needs and results in healthy attachment. This does not mean, as parents and caregivers, we will never occasionally mishandle a situation, such as by making a rude or insensitive comment to our child when we are under great pressure. Circumstances such as these, rather than causing damage to our children, can be utilized as opportunities to model in a healthy form what it is to be human, including appropriate ways of taking responsibility for one's mistakes. It was uncomfortable for me to admit in this book that my unresolved attachment issues still cause me to sometimes respond in ways which are less than healing. This, too, however, is a way of illustrating that the process of trauma recovery is a normal and critically important part of human life. Each of us contributes to healing in the world when we remain open and committed to working through the continuing effects of our own personal traumas.

* * *

Recently, I traveled to Arizona to speak to the San Carlos Apache People about the impact of trauma on society. I had been invited there by Terry Ross, Director of Social Services for the reservation, after we had met at a youth violence conference in San Diego. Terry felt that what I had to say about healing from trauma would be helpful for his people to hear.

The Apache People, like many Native American tribes, have been deeply impacted by trauma, which has been passed on transgenerationally for hundreds of years. The death rate from alcoholism among Native people in the United States is five times higher than among any other group, and the suicide rate on some reservations is more than seven times greater than the rate for the general population. Domestic violence is far too common among Native families, and gang activity is on the rise. While driving through the reservation, I could read the symbolic language of traumatic re-enactment scattered throughout the desolate landscape. Red and blue sneakers and bandanas hung from telephone wires, gang colors announcing their insidious presence, competing with the dull tans and browns of the desert. Everywhere, crudely made signs advertised help for alcoholism, drug addiction, depression, and suicidal thoughts. The ubiquitous nature of these signs was a testament to the desperation of lives trapped in the multi-generational cycle of traumatic re-enactment. Terry told me that San Carlos High School, while isolated and rural, looked exactly like the worst inner city schools, with students expressing their rage through music, clothing, body language, and graffiti.

It is difficult to discuss the effects of historical trauma on a community, cultural group, or nation without becoming involved in potentially divisive political arguments. For this reason, my own thoughts on issues such as blame and ultimate responsibility don't seem useful in this context. Instead, I emphasize that our task here is not to place blame, but rather to understand (utilizing our awareness of the universal human effects of trauma) the impact of specific historical events, and how this impact continues to shape our society today through the trans-generational transmission of trauma.

In the case of Native people, these are the basic historical facts. Their stable and centuries-old society was disrupted by the sudden arrival of the Europeans, an ultimately more powerful outside force. Because of their susceptibility to infectious diseases to which they had never before been exposed (and of which the new arrivals were carriers), the Native population was nearly annihilated by epidemics of devastating illnesses, especially smallpox. Many of those who did not die from disease were killed in armed conflicts as the colonizers exerted increasing dominance and control. They also lost the ability to support themselves, due to new rules of economic competition, in the ways they had for centuries. As time went on, Native society came to bear no resemblance to what it had been before the arrival of the Europeans: they were forced to relocate to reservations; forced to send their children away to boarding schools; forced to abandon their language, cultural heritage, and spiritual practices; and finally, in the interests of assimilation, forced to move once again, this time to major metropolitan areas.

It is easy to see how events of this nature would have an inordinately powerful impact on every individual in the Native community, especially when we remember that, by definition, a traumatic event is one which *overwhelms an individual's ability to cope, rendering them helpless.* Generations ago, the people who lived through these experiences were faced with feelings of immense grief, loss, rage, and helplessness. To compound matters, they were stripped of the support of their traditional society and spirituality, and were therefore unable to work these feelings through to resolution. For this reason, many Native people began, as traumatized humans do, unconsciously re-enacting their trauma through self-destructive and anti-social behaviors, seeking to calm their hyperarousal in any way they could, or splitting off their awareness of unbearable pain through dissociation.

What this situation leads to is generation after generation of parents who are unable, because of their own unhealed trauma, to form healthy attachments with their children. These children then grow up unconsciously seeking to calm their own intolerable feelings of hyperarousal through damaging forms of traumatic re-enactment, without the critical skills needed for effective parenting. This cycle is repeated over and over, ad infinitum, into the future, dragging the unfinished past behind it to sully and tarnish the present.

The tragedy of the soul wound of the Native people is only one example of how the transgenerational transmission of human trauma, through the vehicle of unhealthy attachment, deeply impacts our world. By examining, in a non-political, empathetic, and nonjudgmental manner, how this sequence plays out in the histories of other traumatized communities, cultural groups, or nations, we can obtain a broader view of the overpowering devastation caused by this aspect of human existence. In so doing, we can also come to see that our problems of violence, war, terrorism, and the like, will not be solved by military, political, or diplomatic means alone: but rather by a deep and compassionate understanding of the nature of humanity.

Still Waters

The only voyage of discovery consists not in seeking new landscapes,
but in having new eyes.

—Marcel Proust

CHAPTER SIX

Towards a Healing Society

To put the world in order, we must first put the nation in order; to put the nation in order, we must first put the family in order; to put the family in order, we must first cultivate our personal life; we must first set our hearts right.

—Confucius

Frequently I am asked how I could have given up the practice of medicine after spending so many years (as well as so much money) on training to obtain my degree. It is really very simple: medicine was not my life's work. Once I knew this, I began the lengthy process of extricating myself from the medical profession, while ensuring that Catalyst's HIV/AIDS patients still had the best of care. My true mission, which I put into practice through Catalyst's Creating a Healing Society (CHS) program, is to bring about transformational societal change, which will, one day, result in a world not driven by trauma. That this work is so important to me has much to do with my gratitude for having been able to transcend the horrors of trauma in my life, my regret for the damaging forms of traumatic re-enactment in which I have engaged, and with my desire to help build a world in which others will not have to suffer similarly.

* * *

Some believe that, in times past, the Senoi, an aboriginal people who lived in the jungle highlands of Malaysia, used a process of communal dreamwork which enabled their society to be free of violence and mental illness. Senoi life was said to have revolved around the interpretation of the symbolic language of dreams, which was done each day within individual families and by the larger community. Knowledge gained in this way was then used to guide individuals in their self-development and interpersonal relationships, as well as to deal with matters affecting the community as a whole.

There is controversy as to whether this aspect of Senoi life ever existed, or whether it was the creation of Kilton Stewart, an imaginative adventurer of the 1930's. But true or not, the idea makes intuitive sense: a safe, non-trauma driven society in which everyone, as a community-wide norm, does his or her own emotional work on a regular basis and is adept at reading one's own and others' symbolic language. These are some of the most important elements of what I call a "healing society": one in which we are encouraged and supported, as a normal part of human life, in working through traumatic experiences and difficult feelings, rather than acting them out through self-destructive and anti-social behaviors. It is a way of life, I believe, that would be welcomed by many of us.

Few, if any, large-scale healing societies exist in the modern world. There are, nonetheless, shining examples of progress towards this ultimate goal that can be seen in what are perhaps the unlikeliest of places, even prisons. At the California State Prison/Los Angeles County, the Honor Program is such an example. Proposed by prisoner Ken Hartman (a brilliant man who is one of the most extraordinary human beings I have ever met), its purpose is to create an atmosphere of safety, respect, and cooperation, so that prisoners can do their time in peace, while working on specific self-improvement goals and projects which benefit the community. Prisoners wishing to apply for the program (which is housed on "A" Facility, separate from the rest of the prison) must commit to abstinence from drugs, gangs, and violence, and must be willing to live and work with fellow prisoners of any race. In its first year of operations, there was an 88% decrease in incidents involving weapons and an 85% decrease in violent incidents overall on "A" Facility; the Honor Program saved the California Department of Corrections and Rehabilitation over $200,000 during the first year alone in costs related to the management of violent and disruptive behavior.

I know the Honor Program well, because I spend two days each week there (with my dear friend and colleague Dave Mashore, Director of Catalyst's CHS Program), developing and teaching a CHS course for prisoners and working with Ken Hartman on a variety of CHS expansion activities. It is a remarkable place, in which one can have deep and meaningful conversations with people met at random in the hallways. The level of depth and insight among the participants in our CHS classes, as well as their willingness to look at their own traumatic pasts and other painful matters within themselves, stands in stark contrast to the responses we often observe at the CHS workshops we present in the free world, which are generally more surface and academic in nature, sometimes having a dissociative quality.

Why this should be so is a fascinating question, and one which is vital to ask, because it represents one of the major challenges in creating a paradigm shift in society's mindset regarding the value of introspection. Perhaps it is when we use less painful and more socially acceptable forms of traumatic re-enactment, or when the consequences of our behavior are less clearly connected as cause and effect, we are also less motivated to do the arduous, time-consuming, and often agonizing work of trauma recovery. Because of this, one person, serving a life sentence in prison and tortured by guilt and remorse for a murder committed years ago as a rage and pain-filled teenager, may be driven to find meaning and answers through deep self-examination; whereas another (like my friend Sarah) who believes that her inability to be emotionally present for her children is a minor issue without devastating consequences, may not be willing to invest the time and energy required to do this difficult work.

There are intriguing conclusions to be drawn from this. First, the status quo of our trauma-driven society is actually perpetuated by this "mushy middle" of mainstream individuals: those of us who have found a way to co-exist with the impact of trauma on our lives by utilizing less overtly damaging methods of re-enactment. As they perceive introspection will cause them more pain than they currently are in, these unfortunate individuals engage in socially acceptable and widely available means of distraction, such as television, video games, materialism, and superficial relationships; when distraction alone is not sufficient, tranquilizers and anti-depressants are their preferred modalities for relief of emotional pain. These are the people who must be reached and persuaded that their unconscious responses to trauma are just as damaging as those of a violent criminal: otherwise they will remain a huge obstacle to the changes needed to create a healing society.

Second, I have come to see that the most vital element of leadership in this mission of societal transformation will come from the most unexpected of sources: those of us who have been the most marginalized, and on whom the impact of trauma has been particularly harsh (such as prisoners, drug addicts, and people such as myself who, having been disenfranchised by their own families, view themselves as outsiders). While this may seem counter-intuitive on the surface, to me it makes perfect sense, as I have been privileged to witness the wisdom and power of such exceptional individuals who have had the courage to fully engage in their own journey of healing.

* * *

The seemingly ordinary events of our daily lives often contain profound opportunities to assist those around us in gaining clarity and wisdom, and thus contribute to healing in the world.

When my grandson Christian was six years old, he spent his winter vacation with me. While I was at work, he attended a local day camp run by the City of Palmdale. It was here that Christian had his first experience with peer pressure.

On the second day of camp, when I arrived to pick him up, he was nowhere to be found; this was highly unusual, as Christian was always delighted to see me and usually came running over no matter what activity he was involved in. At the same time that I finally observed him, hiding his face and trying to squeeze his little body as best he could into a corner of the room, the counselor handed me a pink "parent slip" and began to tell me what had happened.

Christian had wanted to play with three older boys that day, who had formed a club with the oldest boy taking the position of "commander." The boys told him that before he could join their club he had to throw sand at a small girl who was playing in the sandlot. Christian had done so.

It was difficult to pry Christian out of his corner, and even when he finally stood up he continued to hide his face in shame. I put my arm around him and we walked out to the car. At first I talked to him of neutral matters, but we were halfway home before he would even consent to make eye contact with me. Then I casually asked the question: "Christian, have you ever heard of peer pressure?"

He shook his head no, but had an interested expression on his face.

"Well, I think you've just had your first experience with peer pressure," I told him.

Then we talked about how human it is to want to be connected with others, a drive so powerful that sometimes we do hurtful things just to feel we are part of a group.

"How did you feel when you threw sand at the little girl?" I asked him.

"I didn't want to do it, and I felt bad about it, but I really wanted to be in that club," Christian explained. "I did tell her I was sorry."

I looked at him affectionately. "This is how we learn," I commented. "We aren't born knowing how to deal with peer pressure.

Now you know, and the next time you will do it differently. We are human; when we make mistakes, we take responsibility for them, apologize to those we hurt, and move on. There is no need to punish ourselves." Christian smiled, all traces of shame gone, and our conversation turned to other things.

The next day, on our way home from camp, Christian told me, "The commander of that club resigned his commission today. He said he didn't deserve to be a commander, because he told me to throw sand at that little girl."

I wondered silently how that boy's parents had dealt with his "parent slip": clearly it had not been the same way I had dealt with Christian's.

"But I told him," he went on, "that we are human, and when we make mistakes, we take responsibility, apologize, and move right on. There's no need to punish ourselves, so he can still be the commander."

"That's awesome, Christian," I replied in amazement. "You will never know what an impact you may have made on that boy, and when he grows up, on his children. What a wonderful person you are."

* * *

Human behavior, and by extension the nature of society, is deeply influenced by the powerful force of peer pressure. In our culture, the pressure is to keep our thoughts superficial, to use methods of distraction to cope with our pain, and to ignore the enormous traumatic elephant charging through our living rooms. To transform society, we must somehow shift the balance of peer pressure, so that it moves in the direction of introspection, working through pain and difficult feelings, and acknowledging the impact of trauma on ourselves and society as an integral part of the human experience. It seems an insurmountable task.

But perhaps not. In his inspired book *The Tipping Point,* Malcolm Gladwell explains it is often the smallest and most surprising details that are essential in creating the critical mass of consciousness that enables transformational change. To disseminate a new idea, Gladwell writes, it is not necessary to reach millions of people through multimedia advertising campaigns, but rather those few special individuals (whom he calls mavens, connectors, and salesmen) who wield the most social power. These exceptional individuals do the work of starting a "social epidemic" which, in our case, would tip the balance of peer pressure to one that makes introspection fashionable and superficiality decidedly out of date.

Finding mavens, connectors, and salesmen to start a healing society epidemic may not be that difficult. Besides my strong spiritual belief in synchronicity (and that we meet those whom we are supposed to for purposes of successfully completing our life journeys), there is also scientific evidence humans are, in fact, exceedingly interconnected. The "small world effect" is a theory that anyone on the planet can be connected to anyone else on the planet through a short chain of social acquaintances. In 1967, sociologist Stanley Milgram conducted an experiment, spawning the now-famous phrase "six degrees of separation," which demonstrated that it took between five and seven intermediaries for a package to reach a stranger in Massachusetts from randomly selected senders in the Midwest. (Recently, Columbia University professor Duncan Watts re-created Milgram's experiment using an e-mail letter as the "package" and confirmed, even in cyberspace, the average number of intermediaries necessary to reach the recipient was, once again, six.)

Christian's story about peer pressure also illustrates the immense power of each of us as individuals when we have healing interactions with others: the effects of which, unbeknownst to us, continue to reverberate for generations to come. Today, healing exchanges such as I had with Christian, and Christian had with his friend, are the exception rather than the norm; but as society shifts towards depth and away from superficiality, the collective force of these individual connections will achieve exponential power and impact.

A friend of mine, who had attended one of the first focus groups for the CHS program, compares me to Don Quixote, frittering my life away in pursuit of unrealistic dreams and ambitions. While I doubt I will see a truly healing society by the end of this lifetime, I am certain the process will have begun towards creating the fundamental change necessary for a more peaceful world. Against seemingly impossible odds, we can transform society. In the optimistic words of *Tipping Point* author Malcolm Gladwell, "With the slightest push—in just the right place—it can be tipped."

Soliloquy

*Your vision will become clear only when you look into
your own heart. Who looks outside, dreams.
Who looks inside, awakens.*

—Carl Jung

CHAPTER SEVEN

Doing Our Own Work

*A truly liberating realization always transcends what went
before, and in bringing us to grasp what was formerly beyond
our reach, the creative leap arises ecstatically, like a momentary
contact with a timeless dimension where everything is
already together and whole.*

—Arthur Egendorf, *Healing from the War: Trauma and
Transformation After Vietnam*

For years, I had equated heart surgery with liberation from the
confinement of my family: and so it was not without inner
turmoil I decided instead to specialize in cancer medicine.
Something about working with dying people resonated deeply within
me, and over time it exerted an inexorable hold. Although I did not
know this consciously then, I was fascinated by the elements of the
grieving process that both death and trauma recovery have in common. Working through the dying process with my patients was a way
for me to have a preliminary view of the path to my own recovery,
a way for me to begin to heal myself while assisting others in their
own healing.

Much later, I realized I had been drawn to Sonny and Frank for
many of the same reasons I had previously been drawn to oncology;
without conscious awareness, I somehow knew connection with
them would bring me closer to the truth of myself. In a trauma-driven
way, I felt safe with Sonny and Frank as I never could with anyone
who bore even a superficial resemblance to my family; but I was also
attracted to their healthy and positive qualities, such as clarity, depth,
and commitment to personal and spiritual growth. As with my cancer
patients, my relationships with Sonny and Frank offered wondrous
opportunities for profound and reciprocal healing.

In the mid-1980's, not long after I began doing my recovery work, I met Richard O'Brien, who had been referred to me for treatment of colon cancer that had spread to his liver. A mortgage banker who loved to work, Mr. O'Brien (as I always called him) was in his mid-forties, married, and had two teenage daughters. He soon became a favorite of everyone in my office because of his love of life, upbeat yet realistic attitude, and desire to take personal responsibility for his medical care. With a disease that was usually rapidly fatal, Mr. O'Brien lived for nearly five years after his diagnosis, during which time we eradicated his cancer with various kinds of chemotherapy and surgical interventions, only to have it recur again and again. After all available standard treatments had failed, he was evaluated for a liver transplant (since that had been the only site of his cancer), and treated with an experimental protocol at a research center in Seattle. In the final year of his illness, unresponsive to any further therapy, the cancer began to grow unchecked in his liver. It was around this time that I got to know his family.

During the last few months of Mr. O'Brien's life, when he was too incapacitated from symptoms of liver failure to come into my office, I would visit him at his home. It was here that I perceived, for the first time in conscious memory, what it must be like to live in a safe family. That safe families actually existed was an astonishing revelation to me: one which laid important groundwork for my recovery from trauma.

While the thought of family had always filled me with horror, and was connected with memories of invasion, disapproval, punishment, and secrets, that was not at all the way it was at Mr. O'Brien's house. Even in the inordinately stressful time of his dying, people treated each other with respect, gave one another space, and talked openly about their feelings without fear of judgment. As his death approached, I spent more and more time there: honored his family would allow me to be a part of something so private and sacred, and grateful for the gift of awareness of that which I never would have believed was possible. However, it would be years before I understood how much I needed to grieve for never having had the safety and love of a family like the O'Briens.

* * *

To change the world, individual transformation must first take place, one person at a time. To create a healing society, those whose lives have been impacted by trauma (and that is the majority of us) must first become aware of this as a hard reality. Then, we must be willing, through the recognition that it will lead to happier lives and a healthier world, to do the difficult work of recovery. Not all of us will embrace this task voluntarily, just as not all of us are disposed to work through our feelings about the death of a loved one, and instead remain mired in destructive denial. Trauma recovery work is not easy, and some of us, no matter what the consequences, will fight all we can to continue in our unconscious and trauma-driven anti-social and self-destructive patterns. For this reason, we must be encouraged to examine the roots of our behavior through the subtle yet powerful influence of societal peer pressure. This is the only way the devastating collective effect of widespread traumatic re-enactment on our world will end.

This peer pressure must also be brought to bear (and perhaps somewhat less subtly) on our current mental health diagnostic and treatment system, which requires a fundamental reform of its own. Among mental health professionals in general, the level of awareness is appallingly low regarding the degree to which traumatic re-enactment influences human behavior. In referring patients for psychiatric care, my experience has commonly been that the outcome of such a visit is the patient is labeled with an often insulting diagnostic term and given medication to alleviate his or her symptoms: and it is left at that. While it is certainly true that some forms of mental illness are biologically based (such as schizophrenia and bipolar disorder) and require medication, in the vast majority of cases, the underlying cause of the patient's distress is unprocessed traumatic experience; even in schizophrenia and bipolar disorder, unhealed trauma can worsen the manifestations of these conditions. Medications, while perhaps necessary in some people for short periods during the most difficult stages of recovery, do not alone heal trauma and will not stop the process of traumatic re-enactment or its impact on society.

In the words of noted traumatologist Dr. Sandra Bloom, "Problems with memory and a tendency to compulsively repeat the past are the hallmarks of trauma." This can be said with total accuracy about the history of psychiatry during the past hundred years. In the late 1800's, psychiatrist Pierre Janet developed most of the precepts of modern trauma theory; however, the ideas of his more famous colleague, Sigmund Freud, came to overshadow Janet's work. It wasn't that Freud did not see patients in his practice whose adult lives were seriously impacted by childhood trauma: on the contrary, he saw a great many of them; but because he could not imagine child abuse (particularly incest) was so prevalent, he instead developed theories focused on the sexual fantasies of children. (That many of his patients were family members of his friends and colleagues further complicated his ability to realistically assess this situation.) For most of the twentieth century, Janet's conclusions were completely ignored. During these years, veterans whose postwar lives were disrupted by the persistent effects of combat were considered cowardly or weak and received little support or respect, sometimes becoming casualties of war long after the war was over. It was not until the Vietnam era that awareness of the human effects of trauma resurfaced and became more widely acknowledged. This was significant progress, but there remains much societal resistance to the idea that we must work through trauma in order to heal. The more popular solution is the quick fix of symptom management, as illustrated by the pervasive advertisements for medications for anxiety and depression, which are promoted as the socially acceptable and appropriate remedy for the problem of human emotional pain.

It is essential to consider why this should be so; I believe the answer lies, once again, in the nature of humanity. Mental health professionals are human, first and foremost, and as such are subject to the same responses to traumatic experience as the rest of us. If we have not worked through our own pain, we find the distress of others particularly disturbing and, consciously or not, prefer to deal with it from as far a distance as possible. If we can make people in pain feel better with medications, at least for the moment, without having to explore with them the darkest places of the human heart: well, perhaps that's not such a bad thing. We are still helping them, after all. Aren't we?

* * *

I often think I belong to a hidden, or at least obscure, community in which things are spoken of that are incomprehensible to most people. We who belong to this cryptic kinship are committed to "doing work" in order to gain power over the impact of trauma on our lives. Our group is eclectic, with people from a great diversity of backgrounds and circumstances; what we have in common, however, is each of us has felt acutely the pain of abuse and trauma, and has been desperate to do whatever it took to find peace. To create transformational change, we must persuade more people to join our number: but what is it exactly that we would have them do?

To me, "doing work" means purposefully taking part in activities designed to make the unconscious conscious; ultimately, it is this process which enables us to overcome the relentless drive to re-enact our trauma. There are other aspects of "doing work" which have to do with recovery from the specific aftereffects of trauma: learning to manage intense emotions; expressing, through safe forms of externalization, feelings which have long been denied; grieving for losses brought about by traumatic experiences; and developing the ability to have healthy boundaries and safe relationships with others. When we work through our issues in these areas, we no longer need to respond to situations in the present as if they were those in the past; we have the clarity to make healthy decisions, and avoid decisions that re-traumatize us as well as society. Rather than continuing to live with shame, through a realistic appraisal of the hardships we have endured we gain respect and compassion for ourselves and for our past need for trauma-driven survival techniques. Once we realize that we, too, have hurt others out of our own pain, we are able to see those who have traumatized us from a new perspective of understanding. Through this work we increase our resiliency, enabling us to bounce back from problems and adversity with even more power than we had before: the ultimate triumph over trauma.

For some of us, it is blatantly clear that we have "work" to do; for others, it may be more subtle. But there are telltale signs in the present that can clue us in to the fact that there may be areas from the past which require our attention: addictive or compulsive behaviors involving drugs, alcohol, food, sex, work, shopping, gambling, or self-injury; difficulties with setting clear boundaries and maintaining healthy relationships; problems with anger and violence; involvement with criminal activities; and chronic anxiety, depression, and low self-esteem. While we may be willing to accept these situations as immutable aspects of our lives (as "the way things are" for us), the truth is that these trauma-driven conditions don't just affect ourselves: they affect us all. The collective effect of millions of individuals "doing their work" and living lives of clarity, self-direction, and purpose will bring about the transformational change we seek: the creation of a healing society, free from the grip of traumatic re-enactment.

While people can be the cause of our worst traumatic experiences, they are, paradoxically, also the essential antidote in our healing. When I look back on the years of my search for answers (before synchronicity intervened and I found Sharon), I see now what

I was missing was a connection with a safe person, one who could be present with me in my pain without expectation or judgment. I have learned that trauma cannot be healed by force of intellect or will alone. While I utilized therapy as my primary path to healing, the close relationships I shared with Sonny and Frank were exceedingly important to my process, as was my deep connection with God and the universe through my personal spirituality.

God's Quarter Acre

There is no enlightenment outside of daily life.
—Thich Nhat Hanh

CHAPTER EIGHT

Trauma and Spirituality

Trauma can be hell on earth; transformed, it is a divine gift.
—Peter A. Levine, Ph.D.

After years of exhaustive efforts to apply my capacities of intellect and will to the problem of trauma recovery, I finally came to understand the paradox of surrender and empowerment.

Not all of my trauma had been of the subtle variety. There was one incident, violent and disturbing, which had haunted me since in flashbacks and nightmares. After doing my recovery work with Sharon for three years, I decided it was time to face up to it.

For several months, I planned a trip back to the scene of this experience. While I knew with great certainty the necessity of this step, my anguish and desperation grew as the day of my departure approached. What lay ahead of me was the confrontation of my deepest pain: the truth of my helplessness and abandonment. I had no idea how I could possibly live with it. I thought I was closer to ending my life than ever before; until, just before I was due to leave, I did the unimaginable.

I surrendered. I gave up my futile quest to find peace through the sole reliance on my human abilities. Sobbing and on my knees, I begged God, the Other Side, and the universe for help.

After that day, help became available to me in the most unexpected and mysterious of ways. Through my spiritual connection, I found meaning in my traumatic experiences which made them not only endurable, but also a source of strength and wisdom. In the perfect and ineffable style of the universe, it was not until I gave up my struggle with helplessness that I gained power over the most painful matters in my life.

During that arduous yet ultimately liberating journey, I found the strength to face the inevitable confrontation with my most profound fear by relying fully on the support of the universe itself. I could not have done this by my own will, as I would not have survived the agony. However, by drawing on the infinite resources of my connection to what is greater than me, I not only survived but prevailed.

By sharing here my personal experience of spirituality, I am in no way implying the specifics of my spiritual beliefs are the only true path to recovery from trauma, or that they should be adopted by anyone other than me. It is for each of us to discover how we relate to a force greater than ourselves, in whatever language we use to describe this, and whether or not we follow a particular religious tradition. Only we can say how we can best utilize the power of spirituality for our own self-actualization and in service to others. My experience is only one such example. Nevertheless, it is my contention and firm belief that spirituality in some form is essential if we are to gain freedom from the destructive cycle of traumatic re-enactment.

* * *

Synchronicity is my primary mechanism of connection with the universe, through which I receive comfort, guidance, and insight regarding the direction and meaning of my life.

In my experience, synchronicity serves several purposes. In times of anguish and uncertainty, a "meaningful coincidence" can merely be a reminder of the presence, love, and support of a power greater than myself. When I receive such a message (which can be as simple as hearing a certain song on the radio at the most appropriate time), I become aware that, although I may be feeling worried and stressed by seemingly arbitrary life events, in reality everything is just as it is supposed to be. I remember that worldly happenings are the symbolic language of the universe, and ask myself, "What is the lesson in this for me?" Through this shift in perspective, I can manage difficult situations with more clarity and peace, regardless of the outcome.

Some forms of synchronicity underscore the need to do a particular piece of trauma recovery work, and occasionally serve as the vehicle through which this work is done. A particularly striking example of this occurred when Frank and I were in Pittsburgh for his evaluation for the liver transplant waiting list. After returning to our hotel room after a day of medical tests, Frank was taking a nap while I read Robert Hopcke's book, *There Are No Accidents: Synchronicity and the Stories of Our Lives.* As Frank slept, I read about one of Hopcke's therapy clients, a man also named Frank, who was struggling with the ongoing impact of his dominating mother on his adult life. The session which Hopcke describes took place during a rainstorm which caused a power failure in his office. Until that day, his client had had litle success in working through this issue; during this session, however, he was finally able to see the problem in a different way. At the moment this epiphany took place, Hopcke writes, "the power went back on, and the office was suddenly, synchronistically, brightly illuminated once again."

As I finished reading this sentence, Frank awoke and began to tell me about the dream he had been having. He was ten years old, had gotten caught for some misbehavior while visiting his uncle's house, and was waiting to find out how his mother intended to punish him. Just as in real life, however, she ignored the entire matter and did nothing about it. Frank told me, "In my dream, I gave my little boy a voice. I said to my mom, 'If you don't set some consequences for me, in the future something terrible is going to happen.'"

Frank was astounded when I showed him what I had been reading at the exact time he had been dreaming. The stunning nature of this synchronicity within a synchronicity enabled Frank to make fully conscious, for the first time, the devastating long-term effects of his abusive childhood.

Perhaps due to their inherently overwhelming nature, death and terminal illness frequently present unique opportunities for synchronistic communication. The circumstances surrounding the passing of my cats, Karate and Toone, provide a poignant and remarkable example that things on this plane of existence are not always as they seem to be.

In 1988, shortly after I began training in martial arts, my Newfoundland dog Kebony brought me an unexpected present. Her excited barking drew me to the back yard just in time to rescue a tiny, black and white, tailless kitten from her exuberant playfulness. Although he never quite trusted Kebony again, the appropriately-named Karate mostly recovered from this traumatic beginning and grew close to me and his three cat-brothers.

Six years later, he met Toone. Bequeathed to me by my friend Cheryl, who was dying of cancer, Toone was an all-black cat who had always been extremely shy, sensitive, and solitary. Cheryl had a special bond with Toone, who rarely left her side throughout her long illness, and it was for this reason she asked me to adopt him after her death. Although her husband loved their cats, Cheryl did not think he felt connected enough with Toone to attend to his special needs. The day after she died, Toone came to his new home with me.

For the next eight years, Toone continued his solitary existence. While he came to love me and appreciate my attention, he steadfastly avoided interaction of any kind with his cat-brothers. He was especially afraid of Karate, who, when given the opportunity, would aggressively seek him out to engage in all sorts of raucous play and general harassment. Because of this, when I was not home to supervise, Toone remained in his own territory (the spare bedroom) with the door closed.

Then, at age twelve, Toone was diagnosed with severe heart failure and cancer of the jaw. Despite his sensitive nature, he adapted to a routine of oral medications, injections, and other home treatments, as well as weekly trips to the vet to have fluid drained from his chest. It was during this time his relationship with his cat-brothers, especially Karate, began to transform.

As his illness progressed, Toone uncharacteristically began to venture out of his private bedroom to spend time in areas of the house frequented by the other cats. I would observe him as he stretched out comfortably in a sunspot on the living room floor, surrounded (though still at a safe distance) by his cat-brothers, and wonder: What is really going on here? Why now after all these years?

Karate had ceased all annoying behavior towards Toone, and was, slowly and imperceptibly, initiating overtures of friendship and closeness. When Toone was seated on one end of the living room couch, Karate would jump up on the opposite end, as far away as possible, and observe Toone's reaction. At first, Toone hissed at him, to which Karate responded by staying where he was and not moving any closer. Over time, Karate, who seemed to understand instinctively Toone's need for gradual desensitization, would sit a little bit closer each time they were together on the couch, stopping only when Toone signaled his discomfort; until, one day, he was close enough to stretch out his leg, touching Toone ever so slightly.

Toone had been ill nearly a year when Karate, fifteen at the time, developed health problems. While these at first seemed minor, over a two-month period his condition deteriorated rapidly, requiring hospitalization in intensive care and emergency surgery for intestinal bleeding. While Karate was in the hospital in critical condition, I brought Toone there for his weekly appointment for his chest fluid tap. As soon as we arrived, however, the surgeon came into the exam room and told me, in a most compassionate way, that Karate had passed on just a few minutes before.

Although I knew how seriously ill he had been, I was unprepared for the suddenness of his death, and was numb and dissociated when they brought his body down from intensive care to the exam room so Toone and I could say goodbye. After some time, when I was ready, another doctor took Toone to the upstairs treatment room for his routine chest tap. Ten minutes later, I heard veterinary staff being paged for an emergency in the upstairs treatment area. I knew at that moment, with absolute certainty, that Toone was gone.

At first, I was shocked by what seemed to be the sheer meaning-less horror of it: two of my beloved cats had died within an hour of each other! But then, as I worked through my grief, and deepened my connection with the Other Side, I began to question what the purpose of such a circumstance could be. The synchronistic timing of Karate's and Toone's deaths caused me to look at the meaning of their remarkable relationship in a different way than I would have had they died months or years apart.

When Toone first became ill, I worried about him because of his timid and sensitive nature. In a practical way, I was concerned the treatments and vet visits would be too much for him; and, strange as this may sound (especially to people who have not experienced closeness with animals), I worried that he would be frightened when his time came to die. However, during the last year of his life, Toone inexplicably allowed himself to become close with Karate, his long-time arch-enemy, and then died with him.

Somehow, Karate and Toone seemed to have the awareness that there was more to their connection than years of surface animosity.

Their synchronistic deaths have caused me to question my human relationships in a similar way, including those which have been the most difficult. Why are certain people in my life? Who are they to me, who am I to them, and what is the real nature of our relationship?

These questions are particularly relevant to my rare but significant experiences of synchronistic meetings with people who play a critical role in enabling me to do particular aspects of my personal growth work. For as long as I can remember, writing has been of the utmost importance to me: however, for years I was consumed with fear at the thought of publication. As a child I had learned it was unsafe to be seen; and while part of me yearned for attention and recognition, another part, the one more firmly in control, felt compelled to hide. Then, in the unlikeliest of circumstances, I met a brilliant writer with whom I developed a close and important friendship. Improbably enough, we soon found we had lived within a mile of one another as children growing up in Brooklyn, and his brother had been in my high school graduating class. These and other synchronistic connections resonated within me, making it possible for me to hear from him things about writing and publication I would have disregarded coming from anyone else. If not for the power of synchronicity, this book might never have been published.

* * *

I advise Christian to question everything, and to take nothing for granted. "The universe can make things on this plane of existence any way it wants to," I tell him. "Why should things be one particular way, and not another? What does it mean that things are exactly the way they are?"

To explore these questions more deeply, Christian and I conduct thought-experiments. We imagine, for example, different ways the world could be structured so that no one has to experience loss of any kind. Perhaps we, and everyone and everything we love, arrive on and depart from this planet at precisely the same instant. Then we ask, what would the world be like without grief? Why does grief exist?

In another experiment, we pose questions about the meaning of the universal human response to trauma. There are, conceivably, other ways, equally advantageous in terms of our survival as a species, in which we could have evolved: why this one, which predestined us biologically to traumatic re-enactment? Why is it necessary for us to heal from trauma, instead of simply being immune to its effects?

The reason, I believe, has to do with the purpose of the healing process itself. When we commit ourselves to healing, whether it is from grief, or trauma, or in preparation for our own death, we will be confronted by profound questions about the meaning of human existence: questions which cannot be answered from our limited perspective. When Sonny learned he had AIDS, after doing everything he could to transform his life, he was driven to know why. Was it punishment for wrongs he had done, or was it a gift through which he could learn deep universal truths? When Frank died in the Liver Transplant ICU, surrounded by patients recovering from their own successful operations, I was desperate for answers. Why could others be saved when he could not? Ultimately, questions such as these lead us into connection with something greater than ourselves; that is, with spirituality. Perhaps it is that grief, trauma, and death serve as generators for our relationship with the divine, and instructors in the art of being human.

When we deal with our pain in a "quick fix" or Band-Aid fashion, we deprive ourselves of the incomparable rewards of self-discovery as we explore our personal spiritual path. It is precisely these rewards: compassion, wisdom, awareness of universal truths, and the ability to use our talents in the service of humanity, which are most needed if we are to create a truly healing society. In the eternal words of poet Robert Frost: "The best way out is always through." Perhaps, it is the only way.

imagine...

Some men see things as they are and say, 'Why?' I dream of things that never were and say, 'Why not?'

—George Bernard Shaw

CHAPTER NINE

Changing the World

We must be the change we wish to see in the world.
—Mahatma Gandhi

When Bobby Maywether was pardoned by Governor Reagan, he was suddenly released back into the free world from San Quentin's Death Row, where he had been imprisoned for the previous twelve years. His burden of unhealed childhood trauma compounded by the violence and cruelty of prison life, it is no surprise that the horror of Death Row did not serve as a deterrent to his immediate return to drugs and crime. Bobby left prison more wounded and traumatized, more in need of calming his unbearable hyperarousal, than he was when he went in. It would take several more years, and only after suffering a serious stroke and heart attack brought about by his use of crack cocaine, for Bobby to begin his spiritual path of healing.

Bobby grew up in New Orleans in a family of successful jazz musicians, always aware that they expected him to carry on their musical tradition. However, Bobby was not interested in jazz; his passion was for drawing. While his artistic talents languished, Bobby forced himself, as best he could, to appear enthusiastic about his musical studies; he loved his family and did not want to disappoint them. As a child he could not communicate in words how oppressed he was by this situation, nor his pain and grief that he did not feel loved and accepted as the unique and special individual he was.

Even as a little boy, his family's lifestyle surrounded Bobby with drugs, alcohol, and prostitution; he had minimal adult supervision and few healthy role models. These circumstances created additional trauma, while also providing easily accessible and often extreme ways for him to express his pain and calm his anguish. At age seven, Bobby began injecting heroin; not surprisingly, this seriously impacted his ability to learn in school. In second grade, an insensitive teacher shamed him in front of the class because of his poor reading skills. Bobby said nothing at the time, but the next day returned to school with a hand grenade he had found in his brother's room. As the teacher stood in front of the room, Bobby rushed up to her with the hand grenade (which he believed to be live), and, in devastating symbolic language, wrapped his arms around her waist, pulled the pin, and waited for them to be blown up.

Even this desperate cry for help went unheard. Bobby was labeled a "disturbed child," but never received any meaningful help in working through the pain which was driving his behavior. There was no one to be present with him without judgment, to ask him, compassionately, what he was trying to say by bringing a hand grenade to school. He grew to become a man consumed by drugs, crime, and violence, and had no awareness why he was this way. No one was surprised when Bobby shot and killed eight people in a drug deal gone bad, and was sentenced to die in the gas chamber at San Quentin.

Bobby had been out of prison and free of drugs for several years when I first met him. He was managing a sober living facility not far from the Catalyst office, and had heard about our work with incarcerated teens. Bobby was interested in what we were doing, and came out to the probation camp with us a few times to see the program in action. Before long, he became an important member of our team, courageously sharing his life experiences with the teens and serving as a clear and compassionate mentor.

Through his personal spirituality and recovery from drug addiction, Bobby had transformed himself into a kind, gentle, and caring man; one who bore no resemblance to the violent and drug-crazed killer who had been sentenced to death. Although he was an intensely private person, I was privileged to know him well, and to consider myself his friend. He rarely spoke about the details of his horrific crimes; however, his remorse was evident in his devotion to works of service and redemption. For the last five years of his life, Bobby was a beloved member of the Catalyst staff, during which time he created hope and healing in the lives of thousands of hurting and traumatized young people. He did this despite the fact that some areas of his life were still deeply impacted by trauma, especially by his experiences on Death Row. (He had confided in me that he could only watch cooking shows on television; anything else carried the risk of causing a horrific flashback of his time in prison.) My friendship with Bobby reminds me still that we don't have to have everything about ourselves perfectly resolved in order to be a force for good in the world.

Bobby's story clearly illustrates that when we make a sincere commitment to the process of personal growth and healing from trauma, we cannot help but contribute positively, in our own unique style and in tangible and practical ways, to the world around us. Consciously or not, we are drawn, through our work of personal healing, to find meaning in our suffering by using our hard-won wisdom in service to others. Bobby did this on many levels, including mentoring thousands of teenagers; being a compassionate presence for hundreds of adults struggling with substance abuse; brightening the day of one co-worker with his supportive and upbeat attitude; and serving as a role model for society that transformational personal change is possible for each one of us, no matter what we may have done in the past.

* * *

When Sonny and I founded Catalyst, we were unaware that we were making visible in the world the results of our own healing. Catalyst became a place where the abstract concepts of personal growth and recovery from trauma were translated into action in the service of others.

For the first several years, I concentrated much of Catalyst's efforts on developing programs for people living with HIV/AIDS. While utilizing my skills as a physician to provide free medical care for patients, I found dedicated and talented people to join the Catalyst staff and implement a broad range of HIV-specific supportive services. On our own and through collaboration with like-minded organizations, we were able to assist our patients with medications, housing, food, transportation, support groups, and even veterinary care and pet food from VCA West Los Angeles Animal Hospital and Karate's and Toone's wonderful veterinarian, Dr. David Bruyette.

Despite the geographic proximity of the Antelope Valley to the cosmopolitan city of Los Angeles, at the time of Sonny's death there was still much ignorance, fear, and outright hostility towards people with HIV within our community. Sonny and I had experienced this on several occasions; one of the most difficult was when he was denied services from a physical therapy facility in Lancaster, on the grounds that his sweat on the exercise equipment would be hazardous to the other patients. HIV/AIDS advocacy, public education, and awareness activities became an important part of Catalyst's early work, with the goal of creating an atmosphere within the community of safety, respect, and compassion for all people, including those living with HIV.

Catalyst embarked on its first advocacy project in 1993, when the family of a man who had died of AIDS reported to us that a local mortuary had refused to accept his body. I contacted the mortician, Jim Mumaw, and listened to his concerns. "I am a single father with two young children," he told me. "I can't take the risk of processing the body of someone who died of AIDS."

"I hear that you are afraid," I replied, "but there are effective precautions you can take to protect yourself. Catalyst can provide a free training program for you and your staff that will teach you about these precautions, so you can all feel more comfortable. It is the law, you know, that funeral directors cannot turn away families of people who died from AIDS."

"Let me think about it," he said. "I'll get back to you."

When, several weeks later, I had heard nothing from him, I followed up.

"I'm sorry," Mr. Mumaw informed me. "I have my family to think about. I'm not going to accept any bodies of people who died of AIDS."

"I'm sorry, too," I responded, "because I have no choice but to report you to the State Board of Funeral Directors and Embalmers for discrimination against people with AIDS."

To my surprise, the case garnered nationwide attention and was covered extensively by the media, including several in-depth articles in the Los Angeles Times. The U.S. Department of Justice became involved, and ultimately issued a ruling that Mr. Mumaw was violating the Americans with Disabilities Act. He was ordered to revise his policies and treat families of people with AIDS the same as he did families of people who had died of other illnesses.

Three years later, Catalyst became involved in another high-profile situation involving HIV prevention education in the Antelope Valley high schools. Frank and I had established a team of volunteers who provided HIV prevention presentations for high school health classes. Trained by Catalyst as health educators, these were dedicated individuals whose lives had been touched by HIV, or were themselves living with HIV. Their personal experiences added a dimension of reality and power to the program, which was especially important in overcoming the attitude of invincibility so common among adolescents. The program, which had been operational for over two years, was very popular and much in demand among students and teachers alike; until one day, the principal of Palmdale High School came into the classroom, interrupted our presentation, and summarily escorted us off the campus.

We soon learned that a student in one of our recent presentations at another high school had complained to her mother about the program. The student felt offended when a question about HIV prevention and oral sex had been asked by a student and answered by the speaker. Her mother was appalled, and immediately went to the School Board to demand the Catalyst program be banned from all Antelope Valley high schools. The Board had ordered there be no more Catalyst presentations pending further investigation.

The public controversy and almost daily media coverage which ensued served to highlight important matters about HIV/AIDS in our community as perhaps nothing else could. Two highly polarized and vocal groups formed: those who believed in offering comprehensive HIV education to all high school students, and those who felt this information should only be taught at home, if at all. For months, both sides battled over this issue in public school board meetings, on radio talk shows, and in letters to the editor. Frank and I became well-known as advocates for HIV prevention; at the same time we created awareness that people with AIDS are human beings who need compassion and respect just like everyone else. As a result of this long period of almost daily media coverage, people who may never have given AIDS a second thought began to consider their feelings about the subject. While Catalyst's program never did get reinstated in the public high schools, over the next few years I could tell the climate regarding AIDS had begun to change. Our patients used to frequently report to us disrespectful interactions with other local medical care providers, but now they just as often told us of caring and kindness during healthcare visits. Catalyst received increasing local support from businesses, corporations, and individuals, enabling us to further expand our services. When the mayor of Lancaster began serving as the Grand Marshal of Catalyst's annual AIDS Walks, I knew we had succeeded in bringing about a significant attitudinal change within our once close-minded community.

We regretted losing our program in the high schools, but the situation carried a hidden benefit: we were now free to devote ourselves more fully to our work with incarcerated youth. What began strictly as an HIV prevention program for these teens evolved in a way which reflected our expanded vision of unhealed trauma as the underlying cause of our most serious social problems. Frank and I recruited and trained many new health educators, people who had re-enacted their trauma through gangs, drugs, and violence, and who were now committed to their own work of personal redemption, healing, and growth. Through education and mentoring, our "Life Challenge" program, as we called it, helped the teens to examine the root causes of their life difficulties: why they were incarcerated, involved with gangs, engaging in violence, and placing themselves at risk for HIV. Continuing to this day, and reaching thousands of incarcerated youth each year, Life Challenge was also the forerunner of the Creating a Healing Society (CHS) program.

In 2003, I held a series of focus groups to help develop a powerful and innovative presentation which would bring the concepts of the CHS program to widespread public attention. Dave Mashore attended the first session with his wife, Debi. Dave and I had been casual acquaintances for nearly twenty years, as fellow students at the Okinawa-Te Karate Organization; in fact, he went to the focus group at the urging of Sensei Richard Triplett, our instructor, who felt Dave and I had similar views of the world and should consider working together.

Dave came up to talk with me after the group was over. "I really feel connected to this work and would love to be more involved," he told me.

At that time, Dave owned a successful worldwide business based in San Diego, where he stayed during the week, returning to Lancaster on weekends to see his family. Nevertheless, he soon began spending an increasing amount of time in Lancaster, working with me to develop the CHS program. Having experienced a difficult childhood, Dave was deeply committed to his own work of healing, through which he had grown to be a profoundly wise and spiritual man. As our work together progressed, I realized Dave had unique insights and ways of viewing the world which complemented mine, and which greatly enhanced the program.

Over the next year, Dave came to see that the CHS program was indeed his life's work. After much soul-searching, prayer, and meditation, he decided to close the business he had painstakingly built over the past ten years. In January 2005, he became an employee of Catalyst, the full-time Director of the CHS program.

Today, Dave and I travel nationwide, reaching thousands of people each year with the concepts of the CHS program. We speak for a wide variety of audiences, including Native Americans, maximum-security prisoners, healthcare professionals, mental health specialists, educators, and the general public. We have raised awareness in churches, schools, substance abuse treatment centers, peace organizations, and many others. Participants are often deeply moved by the CHS program, coming up afterwards to tell us, "You changed my life and my view of the world."

Recently, Dave brought to my attention that Catalyst's very existence, and all the good it has done for so many people over the years, is a direct result of my recovery from trauma. I had been completely unconscious of this connection, but when I thought about it further, I realized it was true. When my life was driven by unremitting emotional pain and constant traumatic re-enactment, I was capable of functioning only in survival mode. During that time, the emotional and spiritual energy and clarity needed to create and nurture Catalyst, to connect with important people to compound the effectiveness of my work, and to understand deeply the concepts of the CHS program, was completely unavailable to me. Only through my work of healing from trauma was I able to see what my life mission was, and to gain the skills to make it a reality.

In this way, the accomplishments of Catalyst can serve as an example of the power within each one of us to create positive change in the world by committing to our own path of healing, and the equally vital task of encouraging and supporting healing in others. The work of Catalyst has made possible medical treatment and caring support for thousands of sick and dying people with AIDS; education, encouragement, and mentoring for tens of thousands of hurting teenagers; and an entire community learning to accept and embrace those whom they previously dismissed as outcasts. As a supportive home base for people like Bobby, Catalyst extends this effect by providing opportunities for others to contribute, in their own unique ways, the tangible benefits of their work of recovery. Through the CHS program, this process is expanded exponentially, as others are inspired to realize the immense power of their personal commitment to healing from trauma.

* * *

When Dave and I first met Eddie Logan, a student in our CHS prison course, he was extremely introverted and shy, rarely speaking to anyone; although he paid close attention in class, he never participated in any group discussions. Nearly two months of the course went by in this way, until after one class, Eddie came up to Dave to ask him a question. After a few minutes of conversation, Eddie said with great surprise, "You know, this is the first time I am looking someone in the eye while talking to them. I have never been able to look anyone in the eye before."

A deeply introspective man, Eddie was determined to find the truth of himself. He wanted to know why his life had taken the direction it had, especially when, in his mind, he had not experienced any significant childhood trauma. Through the CHS program, Eddie learned that seemingly ordinary situations, such as having parents who are often harshly critical of us, can be among the most destructive forms of childhood abuse, especially when the result is pervasive emotional numbing and dissociation from our feelings. One of several children adopted by his parents, Eddie grew up with an alcoholic mother and a quiet and reserved father. His mother often expressed disapproval of her children in a belittling and demeaning manner; Eddie soon came to realize the less he said, the more he could avoid her shaming words. He also knew he could never come out the winner in a match of verbal sparring with her, so it was best he say nothing. This severely curtailed his ability to advocate for himself about things of importance to him, bringing about intense feelings of helplessness and desperation. So painful was this situation that Eddie separated himself from his awareness of these (and any even remotely related) feelings through the unconscious process of dissociation.

Eddie's mother was determined to send her children to a Catholic high school instead of the local public school. Eddie and his siblings definitely did not want to go there; they had heard stories from other teenagers in the neighborhood about the inflexible rules and the cold and uncaring teachers. His older brother, who was much better able to defend himself in debates with their mother, argued with her unsuccessfully about this issue for two years; Eddie knew if his brother wasn't able to change his mother's mind, then he had absolutely no chance of doing so. Having little consciousness of his feelings, and no words to express those he had, as the time approached for him to attend high school he began communicating his message

("I am not going to that school!") through the symbolic language of running away.

Eddie's parents were very concerned about him, but because of their own unresolved trauma they were unable to understand the meaning of his symbolic behavior. They sent him to psychiatrists and psychologists, but without any benefit; as is too often the case with mental health professionals, academic knowledge is no substitute for personal clarity when it comes to the interpretation of symbolic language. Living on the streets when he ran away from home exposed Eddie to some blatantly traumatic experiences, and facilitated his involvement with alcohol and drugs, further increasing his emotional disconnection. Finally, he was incarcerated in juvenile hall, an environment which provided additional trauma and no opportunities for healing.

Eddie grew into a quiet young man who used alcohol to suppress his intense feelings of helplessness and rage. One day, he got into an argument with a woman while he was drunk, and accidentally shot and killed her.

Eddie desperately wanted to know how such apparently "minor" childhood difficulties could culminate in his committing murder. He was deeply serious about using the CHS program as a vehicle for self-examination; this became increasingly evident as the weeks went by and he began speaking up more in class, often staying afterwards to talk with Dave and me. "I've been thinking about my crime, the woman I killed, and what it means to have taken someone's life," he told us one day. "Just like everything else in my life, I was mostly numb about this, too. I'm not there yet, but I'm on the path to really knowing within myself the terrible thing I did, taking responsibility for it, and figuring out what I need to do to make amends."

Several weeks before the course was scheduled to end, Dave and I received an unusual phone call at the Catalyst office. It was from Tanya Jenkins, a producer for KPFK Radio, a popular Southern

California station with a long history of commitment to positive social change.

"I'm calling about the Creating a Healing Society program that you do in the prison," Tanya told us. "Do you have a man named Eddie in your class? He sent me an amazing letter about both of you and your program in the prison. I'd love for you to be guests on The Aware Show; I think our listeners would be fascinated to hear about your work."

Dave and I were at first stunned, then deeply moved. So impacted by trauma as to have been a virtual non-communicator, Eddie had succeeded, through the power of his work of personal growth and healing, in disseminating the message of the CHS program to twenty thousand people.

His transformation did not end there. For the last session of the course, each class member developed a project with the purpose of creating healing within the prison or outside in the free world. As each person came to the front of the room to present their idea, Dave and I wondered whether Eddie would actually stand up in front of the class, or just hand in a written report afterward. When everyone but Eddie had had their turn, Dave asked, "Is there anyone else who wants to share their project?"

To our delight, Eddie got up with a stack of yellow papers in his hand. "I have four projects to discuss," he said. "Do you think we'll have time for all of them?" The class was nearly over, so he was only able to present one. He chose his favorite, a proposal to establish a Toastmasters group, in which prisoners could support one another in developing their skills in public speaking.

On the day of the graduation ceremony for the CHS course, Eddie gave a special present to Dave and me. It was a picture of himself, taken in the prison photo booth; on the back was the inscription, "Enjoying my freedom in Lancaster State Prison. Thank you for helping me find it."

Eddie's story is about the process of reclaiming one's power over trauma and contributing to healing in the world, even from within a maximum-security prison, one of the bleakest and most foreboding environments imaginable. It symbolizes what is possible for all of us: that no matter what our circumstances, or what wrongs we have done out of our own pain, we can free ourselves from the shackles of trauma in our lives, and become leaders in the creation of a truly healing society.

Resources on
Trauma and Recovery

I wrote this book for one purpose: to introduce, in an accessible and humanistic way, the concept of unhealed human trauma as the root cause and driving force of societal and world problems.

There are many excellent books and other resources available with detailed scientific information on subjects such as trauma theory, attachment, and the trans-generational transmission of trauma, as well as wonderful self-help books on what we as individuals can do to heal from trauma. I have listed many of these below, along with workshops, organizations, and websites which may be helpful for those interested in a deeper investigation of the issues discussed in this book.

As in all things, these resources may be helpful for some people and not for others. When considering attending workshops, courses, or other activities, due diligence is critical; speak with the program leaders (and previous participants, if possible) to determine if the workshop or course is safe and appropriate for you. Trust your instincts. (By way of a disclaimer, I have not personally attended all the activities or utilized all the modalities listed here, and cannot be responsible for the outcomes of participation.)

If you have a resource you would like to see in the next edition of this book, or have comments on the ones listed here, please contact me by e-mail: catalyst@qnet.com.

Externalization Workshops

Utilizing techniques developed by Elisabeth Kubler-Ross in her work with the dying, these experiential workshops can be an intense and effective means of working through unresolved trauma. Workshops are led by former staff members of the Elisabeth Kubler-Ross Center, who have had many years of experience in working with survivors of abuse and trauma. Updated information about externalization workshops can be found on the web at www.externalization workshops.com.

• **Safe Harbors 5-day residential workshops,** held twice a year in Los Angeles, CA and in Durham, NC. Contact Sharon Tobin, LCSW at (818) 845-0729 or 2312 W. Olive Street, Suite B, Burbank, CA 91506.

• **Growth and Transition 3-day workshops** in Tucson, AZ. Contact Ann Taylor Lincoln at (520) 325-3100; e-mail: LJLATL@ hotmail.com; or 2630 N. Santa Lucia, Tucson, AZ 85715.

• **The Safe Center,** Boulder, CO. Contact Lea Abdnor, (303) 494-0280, e-mail: Abdnor@safecenter.com.

• **Moving through Loss and Transition Workshops** in the San Francisco Bay area. Contact Roz Leiser at Life Transitions Network, (415) 263-4822; e-mail: griefworkshops@aol.com; P.O. Box 31579, San Francisco, CA 94131; website www.transitions workshops.com.

• **Life, Loss, and Healing Workshops** are held at Avila Retreat Center, Durham, NC. Contact the Center at (919) 477-1285; 711 Mason Road, Durham, North Carolina 27712; or contact Nancy Mullins at (413) 268-7342; e-mail: DavidandNancy@Mullins.info.

• **Compassion Fatigue and Burnout Workshops** for animal control officers, animal shelter staff, and veterinary practices are conducted nationwide by Nancy Mullins and Roz Leiser. They also lead

1-day Pet Loss Workshops. Contact Carol Brothers at (410) 987-5164; e-mail: Carol_AB@juno.com; or at 1333 Sweet Pea Path, Crownsville, Maryland 21032.

- **Where We Have Been—Where We Are Going,** a 4-session program exploring end of life issues. Contact Nancy Jaicks Alexander at Compassionate Seeing, (510) 681-6284, or P.O. Box 5534, Berkeley, CA 94705.

- **For workshops in the United Kingdom,** contact Helen Rickard at Albertine, 48 Saxon Road, St. Werburghs, Bristol BS2 9UG, England; 011-44-117 954 1268; Fax: 011-44-117 955 5900; e-mail: helen.rickard@ukonline.co.uk. Contact Nick Price at 14 Egypt Mews, Morningside, Edinburgh EH10 4RS, Scotland; e-mail: nickprice9@compuserve.com; or Phyllida Anam-Aire by e-mail: anamaire@celtic-healing.com.

- **For workshops in Spain,** contact Alba Payas, Servei de Suport al Dol de Girona, Sta Eugenia 172, 17006 Girona, Spain; office: 011-34-972-244441; home: 011-34-972-231767; or by e-mail: apayas@grn.es, or serveidolgirona@eresmas.com.

- **For workshops in The Netherlands,** contact Rochelle Griffin, Vuurvlinder, Hogestraat 30, 6624 BB, Haarewaarden, The Netherlands; 011-31-487-57-3378.

- **For workshops in France,** contact Herve Mignot, EKR France, 27, quai Tilsitt, 69002 Lyon, France; 011-33-47-240-2710; e-mail: mignot.h@wanadoo.fr; website: www.EKR.France.free.fr.

- **For workshops in Germany,** contact Phyllida Anam-Aire or Helga Herms, Pelzetleite 65, D-90614, Ammerndorf, Germany; 011-49-9127-6705.

- **For workshops in New Zealand,** contact Liese Groot-Aberts, 15 Empire Avenue, Enclosure Bay, Waiheke Island, New Zealand; 011-64-9-372-6601; fax: 011-64-9-372-6618. Also contact Hetty Rodenburg, 42 Kotari Road, Days Bay, Eastbourne, New

Zealand; 011-64-4-562-7475; fax: 011-64-4-562-0022; e-mail: hetty rodenburg@xtra.co.nz.

• **For workshops in Australia,** contact Keith Taylor, 79 Turpentine Street, Wyoming 2250, New South Wales, Australia; 011-61-24-328-4519. Also contact Sue Marsden, 11 Sheridan Crescent, Stanwell Park, New South Wales, Australia; 011-61-24-294-8636; e-mail: Smarsden47@hotmail.com.

Other Workshops/Courses

• **Kari Joys, M.S. Choosing Lightheartedness Personal Growth Workshops,** Coeur d'Alene, Idaho; website: www.kari-joys. com; (509) 534-7374.

• **The Center for Nonviolent Communication;** Marshall Rosenberg, Founder. Offers workshops worldwide on the practical techniques of nonviolent communication and effective conflict resolution; website:www.cnvc.org; (818) 957-9393.

• **Vipassana Meditation Courses.** Vipassana means "To see things as they really are." Provides free courses worldwide for adults, teens, and children on the techniques of Vipassana meditation. Main website: www.dhamma.org; local contacts can be found on this site.

• **Peter Alsop, Ph.D.** A nationally known singer/songwriter, educator, and humorist, Peter's award-winning music is widely used by parents, teachers, and others to help children discuss sensitive topics. His website, www.peteralsop.com, has information on his concerts, workshops, trainings, and more.

Organizations

CommunityWorks

Community Works provides consultation, education, and organizational development programs to reduce conflict and violence in schools, workplaces, and mental health treatment environments. Their website, www.sanctuaryweb.com, has excellent articles about the basics of trauma theory, as well as about the impact of unhealed human trauma on society and the world.

The Foundation for Human Enrichment

7102 La Vista Place, Suite 200
Niwot, CO 80503
(303) 652-4035
www.traumahealing.com

A nonprofit organization, the Foundation is dedicated to worldwide healing and prevention of trauma. It provides professional training in the Somatic Experiencing ® technique of healing from trauma, as developed by Dr. Peter Levine.

The Institute for Attachment and Child Development

P.O. Box 730
Kittredge, CO 80457
(303) 674-1910
www.instituteforattachment.org

The Institute provides treatment for children and families impacted by attachment issues, as well as education and training for the general public and mental health professionals.

The Institute for Psychohistory

140 Riverside Drive

New York, New York 10024

(212) 799-2294

www.psychohistory.com

This website is interesting because it focuses on the relationship between "the emotional origin of the social and political behavior of groups and nations, past and present," i.e., the impact of human trauma on historical events. However, my inclusion of this resource here does not constitute my agreement with or endorsement of any political views expressed by the Institute for Psychohistory.

The Lionheart Foundation

P.O. Box 194, Back Bay

Boston, MA 02117

(781) 444-6667

www.lionheart.org

This nonprofit organization works to "redefine prisons as places of healing and rehabilitation." The agency sponsors the National Emotional Literacy Project for prisoners, and the National Emotional Literacy Project for at-risk youth. Their publication, *Houses of Healing: A Prisoner's Guide to Inner Power and Freedom,* is provided free of charge to prisoners throughout the country.

The Sidran Institute

200 E. Joppa Road, Suite 207

Towson, MD 21286 USA

Phone: 410-825-8888

Fax: 410-337-0747

www.sidran.org

The Sidran Institute is a national nonprofit organization devoted to helping survivors of trauma, as well as providing education and advocacy about traumatic stress. They provide referrals to therapists and other resources for healing from trauma.

The Trauma Center at Justice Resource Institute

1269 Beacon Street
Brookline, MA 02446
(617) 232-1303
www.traumacenter.org

The Trauma Center provides education and treatment for trauma survivors, and training for mental health professionals.

Books and Articles

Bass, Ellen, and Davis, Laura (1994). *The Courage to Heal—Third Edition—Revised and Expanded: A Guide for Women Survivors of Child Sexual Abuse.* New York: HarperCollins Publishers.

Bloom, Sandra, and Reichert, Michael (1998). *Bearing Witness: Violence and Collective Responsibility.* Binghamton, New York: The Haworth Maltreatment and Trauma Press.

Bloom, Sandra (1997). *Creating Sanctuary: Toward the Evolution of Sane Societies.* New York: Routledge

Danieli, Yael (Ed.), (1998). *International Handbook of Multigenerational Legacies of Trauma.* New York: Plenum Press

Davis, Laura (1990). *The Courage to Heal Workbook: A Guide for Women and Men Survivors of Child Sexual Abuse.* New York: HarperCollins Publishers

Davis, Laura (1991). *Allies in Healing: When the Person You Love was Sexually Abused as a Child.* New York: HarperCollins Publishers

Davis, Laura (2002). *I Thought We'd Never Speak Again: The Road from Estrangement to Reconciliation.* New York: HarperCollins Publishers

Egendorf, Arthur (1986). *Healing from the War: Trauma and Transformation after Vietnam.* Boston, MA: Shambhala Publications

Gil, Eliana (1983). *Outgrowing the Pain: A Book For and About Adults Abused as Children.* New York: Dell Publishing

Goleman, Daniel (2005). *Emotional Intelligence: 10th Anniversary Edition; Why It Can Matter More Than IQ.* New York: Bantam

Hartman, Kenneth (2004). *A Prisoner's Purpose.* The Power of Purpose Awards 2004: The Winners of a Worldwide Essay Competition (pp. 144–154). New York: Cosimo Books

Hartman, Kenneth, "Seeking Peace." *Whole Life Times,* December 2004. http://wholelifetimes.com/2004/wlt2612/backwords2612.html

Joys, Kari (2006). *Choosing Light-Heartedness: A 33-Day Journey to Overcome Anxiety, Depression, and Dysfunctional Family Issues.* Spokane, WA: Higher Consciousness Books

Keyes Jr., Ken (1989). *The Hundredth Monkey.* Coos Bay, OR: Vision Books

Kubler-Ross, Elisabeth (1969). *On Death and Dying.* New York: Touchstone Press

Kubler-Ross, Elisabeth (1974). *Questions and Answers on Death and Dying.* New York: Touchstone Press

Kubler-Ross, Elisabeth (1975). *Death: The Final Stage of Growth.* New York: Touchstone Press

Kubler-Ross, Elisabeth (1981). *Living with Death and Dying.* New York: Touchstone Press

Kubler-Ross, Elisabeth (1983). *On Children and Death*. New York: Touchstone Press

Kubler-Ross, Elisabeth (1987). *AIDS: The Ultimate Challenge*. New York: Touchstone Press

Kubler-Ross, Elisabeth (1995). *Death Is of Vital Importance: On Life, Death, and Life After Death*. Barrytown, New York: Station Hill Press

Levine, Peter and Frederick, Ann (1997). *Waking the Tiger: Healing Trauma: The Innate Capacity to Transform Overwhelming Experiences*. Berkeley, CA: North Atlantic Press

Levine, Peter (2005). *Healing Trauma: A Pioneering Program for Restoring the Wisdom of Your Body*. Boulder, CO: Sounds True, Inc.

Levine, Peter (2005). *Healing Trauma: A Pioneering Program for Restoring the Wisdom of Your Body* (Sounds True Audio Learning Course). Boulder, CO: Sounds True, Inc.

Lew, Mike (2004). *Victims No Longer: The Classic Guide for Men Recovering from Sexual Child Abuse*. New York: HarperCollins Publishers

Lozoff, Bo (1985). *We're All Doing Time: A Guide for Getting Free*. Durham, NC: Human Kindness Foundation

Miller, Alice; Hannum, Hildegard (Translator); and Hannum, Hunter (Translator) (1990). *For Your Own Good: Hidden Cruelty in Child-Rearing and the Roots of Violence*. New York: The Noonday Press

Miller, Alice (1997). *The Drama of the Gifted Child: The Search for the True Self*. New York: Basic Books

Miller, Alice; deMause, Lloyd (Preface); Hannum, Hildegard (Translator); and Hannum, Hunter (Translator) (1998). *Thou Shalt Not Be Aware: Society's Betrayal of the Child*. New York: Farrar, Straus, and Giroux

Miller, Alice; and Jenkins, Andrew (Translator) (2005). *The Body Never Lies: The Lingering Effects of Hurtful Parenting*. New York: W. W. Norton & Company

Ross, Gina. (2003). *Beyond the Trauma Vortex: The Media's Role in Healing Fear, Terror and Violence.* Berkeley, CA: North Atlantic Books.

Shapiro, Robin (Ed.) (2005). *EMDR Solutions: Pathways to Healing.* New York: W. W. Norton & Company

Van der Kolk, Bessel; McFarlane, Alexander; and Weisaeth, Larry (1996). *Traumatic Stress: The Effects of Overwhelming Experience on Mind, Body, and Society.* New York: The Guilford Press

Wiesenthal, Simon (1998). *The Sunflower: On the Possibilities and Limits of Forgiveness.* New York: Schocken Books

Websites

• *The Adverse Childhood Experiences (ACE) Study: The Effects of Adverse Childhood Experiences on Adult Health and Well Being.*

This is a decade-long and ongoing collaboration between Kaiser Permanente's Department of Preventive Medicine in San Diego, California, and the Centers for Disease Control and Prevention. Full information at www.acestudy.org.

• *The Compulsion to Repeat the Trauma: Re-enactment, Revictimization, and Masochism,* by Bessel van der Kolk, M.D., Psychiatric Clinics of North America, Volume 12, Number 2, Pages 389–411, June 1989. Detailed and excellent academic article about traumatic re-enactment. View online at http://www.cirp.org/library/psych/vanderkolk/.

• *The Political Trauma Vortex* by Gina Ross, MFCC. A fascinating, unbiased, and non-political discussion of the trans-generational effects of trauma and its impact on world events, with special emphasis on the Middle East conflict. View online at http://www.ginaross.com/publications.html. Other articles of interest at this same website include *Emotional First Aid Brief Guide, The Trauma Vortex in Action Again in the Middle East,* and *The Media and the Understanding of the Trauma Vortex at the Political Level.*

The Creating a
Healing Society Program

If you have been inspired by this book, and would like to learn more about how unhealed trauma impacts society and the world (and how you can help make transformational social change), consider bringing the Creating a Healing Society program to your community. Powerful and revolutionary, Creating a Healing Society presentations, workshops, trainings, and keynote addresses are tailored to the specific needs of our diverse audiences.

For more information on the Creating a Healing Society program, or to purchase additional copies of this book, please visit our website at www.creatingahealingsociety.org. Contact Dave Mashore at The Catalyst Foundation for details about customized training programs, workshops, conference presentations, keynote addresses, and more; he can be reached by phone at (661) 948-8559 x 112, or by e-mail at davem@qnet.com.